D1084606

Renaissance Humanism
Studies in Philosophy and Poetics

meðieval & renaissance texts & studies

Volume 51

Center for International Scholarly Exchange
Columbia University
International Studies, Volume 1

Renaissance Humanism
Studies in Philosophy and Poetics

BY

Ernesto Grassi

medieval & renaissance texts & studies
Binghamton, New York
1988

Translated from the German *Einführung in philosophische Probleme des Humanismus* (Darmstadt: Wissenschaftliche Buchgesellschaft, 1986) by Walter F. Veit, Monash University.

ISBN 0–86698–035–0 (alk. paper)

· This book is set in Bodoni typeface,
smythe-sewn and printed on
acid-free paper to library specifications.
It will not fade, tear or crumble.

Printed in the United States of America

In memoriam

Martin Heidegger

Contents

Foreword

This volume is the third of Ernesto Grassi's challenging and controversial studies of Renaissance Humanism to be published by MRTS, forming a kind of triptych in our series. The first panel of that triptych was *Heidegger and the Question of Renaissance Humanism: Four Studies,* which we published in 1983 (MRTS Volume 24); the second, *Folly and Insanity in Renaissance Literature* (MRTS Volume 42, 1986), was written in collaboration with Maristella Lorch.

This volume is also the first in an occasional series undertaken in collaboration with the Center for International Scholarly Exchange at Columbia University. The aim in both respects is the same — to explore, from a fresh vantage point, important questions in those earlier cultures which remain the most stimulating international source of our intellectual and spiritual heritage.

Many scholars helped to bring this work into print. Professor Grassi's and my dear and endlessly generous friend, Maristella Lorch, Director of the Center for International Scholarly Exchange, was an animating force behind the entire project of these three books. Professor Walter Veit of Monash University translated the German version, with assistance from Silke Beinssen-Hesse and Stephen Jeffries. Michael Pavese edited the translation with immense care and scrupulous attention to the problems of clarifying complex concepts. Michael Horan checked and edited all the quotations in the text and all the notes.

Given the interlocking character of the argument, there is no formal index; instead, the table of contents provides a detailed guide to the main sections of the work.

M. A. Di Cesare
February 1988

Renaissance Humanism
Studies in Philosophy and Poetics

Freiburg 1929: Heidegger

THE PRESENT ESSAY IS DEDICATED TO THE MEMORY OF MY TEACHER, Martin Heidegger. My first scholarly work was written under his supervision, and when published in 1932 in Italy (*Il problema della Metafisica platonica*), it was also dedicated to him. With respect to the problem of the philosophy of Humanism in its relationship to antiquity, and to Heidegger's critique of the philosophical import of Humanism, this essay aims to complete a circle.

The following pages may seem to be only autobiographical in character, but they are closely linked to the discussion of the problem of Humanism and its topicality during the historical events of the last fifty years. They are, not least, a documentation of a period which has been decisive for occidental philosophy. They point to the intimate connection, all too often forgotten, between the personal experience of a time and the theoretical problems which arise out of it. The aim of the following discussions is to identify the specific nature of the philosophy of Humanism.

Surprisingly, the question of the essence of the speculative tradition of Humanism is intimately connected to the question of the relationship between Italian and German philosophy. During the years 1864–65 the journal *Der Gedanke* had a permanent correspondent in Naples who reported

on the developments in Hegelian philosophy in Italy and especially in
Naples. F. de Sanctis (1817–83), who in 1861 became Italy's first minister
for culture, translated Hegel during his detention in the Castel dell'Ovo.
In this context, Spaventa's publication on the relationship between Italian
and European philosophy is decisive. Spaventa's thesis was that the importance of Italian philosophy for Europe begins with Humanism and the
Renaissance, and that this tradition is extinguished at the stakes of the
Inquisition. For this reason, the tradition continued only in freer coun-
tries, such as Germany. Indeed, Spaventa maintains that German idealism was the heir to that theoretical tradition and had, in fact, developed
it further:

> Italian philosophical thought was not extinguished at the stakes of
> our philosophers, but continued to grow in freer regions and among
> freer minds: hence the search for it in its new fatherland in Germa-
> ny is not a servile imitation of German philosophy. Spinoza, Kant,
> Fichte, Schelling, and Hegel are the true disciples of Bruno, Cam-
> panella and Vico.[1]

In accordance with this thesis, we shall here discuss and evaluate the
philosophy of Humanism as the preparatory stage of Renaissance philosophy
on the one hand, and, on the other, locate it within the framework of the
problematic of German idealism and theory of knowledge. It is also illuminating to be reminded of Croce's idealistic interpretation of Vico, in whose
thoughts the essence of humanistic philosophy was summarized and evaluated for the last time in the eighteenth century, or of Gentile's understanding of Humanism, or of Cassirer's essays on the problematic of epistemology
in relation to the philosophy of Humanism and of the Renaissance.

And in this context there also arose the still widely accepted thesis that
the essence of humanistic philosophy is to be sought for and to be found
in a renewed Platonistic thought – as in Marsilio Ficino, Pico della Mirandola, or Diacceto. One of the best known representatives of such an historical
and theoretical interpretation is Paul Oskar Kristeller.

To discuss the problematic outlined and developed in the present investigation, it is necessary to make one further point. In accordance with his
scheme of the history of philosophy, Hegel set up a double thesis: if in
the realm of philosophy a nostalgia for the past were permissible, it would
have to be a longing for the philosophy of antiquity and for Greek philosophy
in particular. But because the philosophy of antiquity stands only at the

beginning of metaphysical thought and because the dialectic of the development of philosophy has arrived at a much broader problematic, it is not possible to stay with those beginnings of philosophy. Such a view leads implicitly to Hegel's assertion that Humanism, which, because of its Platonism and Neo-Platonism, goes back mainly to the metaphysics of antiquity, can demand only a *historical* rather than a theoretical interest. This thesis is strengthened through Hegel's critique of Humanism (which we shall have to come back to), particularly through his assertion that the philosophy of Humanism had remained caught in imaginative and metaphoric thinking, and that because of this it was incapable of lifting itself to the level of pure conceptual and rational thought. But again this reinforces the thesis that the discussion of the philosophy of Humanism is mainly of historical interest, or, rather, that the discussion remains outside the really decisive theoretical problems of contemporary philosophy.

In the context of this negative evaluation of historical interest (i.e., within the frame of phenomenology which was dominant during the thirties), I would like to refer to a personal experience. I do not mention it for autobiographical reasons, but because it is of symptomatic significance for the philosophical situation of that time.

In 1924, shortly before completing my studies with my venerated teacher at the University of Milan, Piero Martinetti, I visited Freiburg in order to visit Husserl, who, at that time, was the acknowledged authority of Western philosophy. In those days the wife of the university professor was considered to be the only competent person—far more so than his assistant—able to decide whether someone was worthy of a conversation with the master. Frau Malvine Husserl examined me thoroughly for three quarters of an hour to see whether I would stand up to the discourse. Finally, the meeting with the master took place. I was allowed to ask questions and I received helpful hints for my work. All of a sudden, Husserl passed the following verdict: "Young man, as an Italian you are particularly predestined for philosophy. Work on steadily, without haste, and you will succeed."

I was surprised and asked Husserl what made him come to that conclusion. He answered: "Because you Italians approach the phenomenon itself; because of your sense for the concrete in philosophy; you do not start from abstract, *apriori* thinking and systematic historic schemata as do we German philosophers." Upon my reply that contemporary Italian philosophy was mainly concerned with a renewal of the systematic and historic philosophy of Hegel, because of the idealistic tradition of Spaventa, Croce and Gentile, in which I had been educated, the master retorted: "Young man, if you have been brought up within the frame of such a problematic then you are lost and there is no hope for you."

In the context of the problem of Humanism, I shall now turn to consider my relationship with Heidegger, to whom this essay is dedicated. Here, too, I must refer to autobiographical incidents. They form part of the discussion about the development of the philosophical significance of Humanism and, furthermore, contribute to the question of Heidegger's negation of the speculative importance of Humanism.

In 1928, after a short time spent with Scheler and Jaspers, I went to Heidegger in Marburg. He agreed that I should work under his guidance. When in 1929 he took over the chair of philosophy at Freiburg, I also moved to that university, first as lector, then as lecturer, and, finally, as associate professor. I have already mentioned that my habilitation thesis on "The Problem of Plato's Metaphysics," which was presented in 1931 at the University of Rome, was written under Heidegger's guidance and was, therefore, dedicated to him. Benedetto Croce simply handed my book on to his publisher, Laterza. At that time the name of the man to whom it was dedicated meant nothing to him. Some years later, Croce would never have recommended a work with that dedication to his publisher. He not only rejected Heidegger's theories, he radically (and rightly) rejected Heidegger's political stance.

I should like to refer briefly to that time at Freiburg University, which appears almost mythical to us today, in order to emphasize the essential differences between university life then and the bureaucratic nature of university life today. Among the luminaries of the philosophical faculty at the time were people like Husserl, who was giving his last lectures, Heidegger, who had just been called to take the chair, Hugo Friedrich, the great Romance scholar whose *Structure of Modern Lyrics* I was to publish later, Schadewaldt, the classical philologist, Eucken, the famous economist, and Wilhelm Szilasi, whom Heidegger had asked to conduct seminars and of whom Heidegger told me then that he was the one and only person who really understood him. Not only were Heidegger's lectures unforgettable, but also his seminars. I mention only his seminars on the third book of Aristotle's *Metaphysics*. Participants in these seminars were, among others, Bollnow, Lotz, and Müller; at his lectures I saw Zubiri and often, although sporadically, Ortega.

But to return to my topic. Already in his lectures I was surprised by Heidegger's critical attitude, always present in the background, towards everything connected with the Latin tradition. To me, coming from Italy or, rather, influenced by the teaching of Croce and Gentile, Heidegger's interpretation of Greek philosophy was a revelation. From the standpoint of theory, Greek philosophy was hardly relevant to me, except for its purely historical importance. New horizons were opened by Heidegger's discussion of the problem of ἀλήθεια [truth] as the question of unconcealedness. To him this was the original question of philosophy. But I was puzzled by Heidegger's latent polemical attitude towards the Latin philosophical tradition, which represented for him a specific misinterpretation of the original Greek thought. He maintained that Latin philosophy had remained within the framework of the traditional metaphysics of being. I do not wish to discuss this thesis here any further because it will be debated sufficiently later in the course of the essay. The problem of truth as enunciated by traditional metaphysics implies as its philosophical starting point the duality of subject and object, both as beings, and it implies, therefore, a metaphysics which arrives at the basic problem of a first, original and highest being, which is to be determined rationally and causally: metaphysics as theology. This attitude of Heidegger's—which arose from his discussion of the problem of the ontological difference—and his fundamental thesis that traditional metaphysics did not originally consider the problem of Being and was, therefore, destined to forget the Problem of Being, forced me more and more to investigate the problem of the philosophical relevance of my own Latin and humanistic tradition insofar as it was rooted in a renewed platonism with a Christian character.

Despite these questions, which preoccupied me a great deal at the time, we need to be reminded today of the atmosphere of those early semesters at Freiburg which began in 1929 and then changed completely in 1933. The atmosphere at the university then, and the prophetic words which Husserl uttered to me during this occasion and which still ring in my ears, can perhaps be conjured up by an episode. In the academic life of those years the Dean's Ball was still a major event, and the one to which I refer happened during the deanship of the art historian Jantzen. Usually, the Dean's Ball consisted of a dinner for the members of the faculty and their wives, followed by a dance. But the invitation to the ball in question, announced, surprisingly, also a talk by the dean on "The Photographic Portrait in the Twenties." Such an invitation, I have to admit, aroused a slight feeling of weariness: why should the Dean's Ball be burdened with a lecture? But what—to the great astonishment of the guests—did the lecture consist of? Secretly, Jantzen had obtained from the wives of all members of the faculty photographs of their husbands. During his lecture he began to screen and to interpret all the photographs: Husserl as a k.u.k. gunner; Heidegger among Catholic priests; the art historian Bauch as a naval cadet; I figured in, sitting under the vibrating shadows of an olive tree in Tuscany, as an example of early expressionism. Jantzen, of course, put the main emphasis on the appropriate interpretation of the characters of the people portrayed.

At the end of the lecture, Husserl took me aside and said—I shall never forget his words—almost prophetically: "You are young, you are a foreigner, imprint on your memory this image of a humane university life in Germany; it may be that one day all this will vanish and only an eye-witness will be able to report on it." Was Husserl referring to the nascent National Socialism? I can hardly believe it, for I remember a dinner with Heidegger in 1930 to which Husserl, Szilasi and his wife, my wife and I were invited and during which no mention was made of National Socialism. And suddenly, indeed without warning, the picture changed tragically at the beginning of the summer semester of 1933. The same Jantzen now professed National Socialism; Schadewaldt, the classical philologist whom I had met at Nervi in March and who confessed to be dismayed by the course of political events, started his lectures in the summer semester by praising the beginning of a "new era" in German history. Every meeting with people whom one had thought of as intimate friends or colleagues was under a cloud of silence where the divisive political events were concerned.

Heidegger professed National Socialism. It was not so much a political as a philosophical decision, one of principle. He was of the opinion that forgetfulness of Being as the essence of traditional metaphysics was necessarily leading to the demise of occidental thought. For this he held Anglo-Saxon and Marxist philosophy responsible, and he believed the demise could be overcome by the ideology of National Socialism. Without referring to his notorious inaugural address as rector, it is sufficient to remember assertions made during his lectures on Hölderlin in 1941—that is, at a time when his rift with the Party had become apparent. In the interpretation of Hölderlin's hymn "The Ister" he also mentions the consequences of forgetting for the problem of Being. He points out that pure rational thinking leads to an absence of measure "which is the principle of that which we call Americanism; Bolshevism is only a sub-species of Americanism. The really dangerous form of such thinking arises in the shape of democratic civil society mixed with Christianity, and all that in an atmosphere that distinctly lacks a sense of history."[2]

In a footnote to the same lecture his negative opinion about the Latin tradition appears again. We read: "The character of Germans [Eigentum der Deutschen] does not need the pompous display and the loud gestures and the irritating noises and the giant monuments of the un-German reminiscent of the Romans and Americans."[3] Starting from the relationship between Greekness and Germanness, he takes a negative and polemical attitude towards Humanism, maintaining that the relation between Greekness and Germanness "does not suffer any assimilation and balancing. Hence the merely 'humanistic' connections and revivifications (Renaissance) are caught up in the margins of historicity."[4] Even in 1941, Heidegger speaks of the historical "uniqueness of National Socialism."[5]

In the lecture mentioned above, Heidegger sums up perhaps most unambiguously the theoretical connection between his political stance and the problem of Being in the following sentence:

> Man is a ζῷον πολιτικὸν because he, and only he, is a ζῷον λόγον ἔχον, a living being who possesses the word, that is to say a being who is capable of addressing being as such with regard to its Being. Who, or what, man is *cannot be decided 'politically'* in the sense of the thinker who calls man a 'political' being because the essence of the πόλις is determined in relation to the essence of man (*and because the essence of Man is determined by the truth of Being!*).[6]

For that reason a political decision can and may be discussed and understood only through the philosophical understanding of Being, that is, in the light of the ontological difference. This is the theoretical presupposition of his inaugural speech, which he held, surrounded by burning candles, in a near-mystical atmosphere. Then followed the break with his Jewish friend Szilasi, who had moved to Switzerland. During his tenure as rector Jewish books had been dragged on oxcarts to the front of the University and burned. With regard to Heidegger's attitude towards the Jews it is not sufficient to mention again the fact that he did not participate in the funeral of his teacher and patron Husserl. I also remember what he told me before he made any of his official declarations on matters of political and philosophical principle. It was still 1932, and I asked him why he

did not force his Jewish students who had been members of his seminar
for years to finish their doctoral theses as soon as possible in order for
them to escape the dangers which had already appeared on the horizon.
He answered that he did not wish to be compromised by them and that
they should transfer to Professor Honecker, then Catholic philosopher at
the University of Freiburg.

My relationship to Heidegger became more and more distant. I wish
only to mention a final episode which is revealing of his character. It was
during the time when he had already fallen into disgrace with the National Socialists and had been forced to resign as rector. It happened during
an evening in his former house on the Rötebuckweg: an electrical storm
had gathered; his study—looking towards the hills—was in half-darkness,
and lightning flashed over the Black Forest. To start, I asked him how
he was. He answered: "Bad." I asked him whether the reason lay in his
recent bad relationship with the Party. His answer was: "Certainly, but
not only because of that. Rather it is because I have been removed as
member of the advisory committee of the Nietzsche archive." Whereupon
I congratulated him, for to my knowledge Reinhard and W. F. Otto had
shortly before been expelled also. His verbatim response was: "No, matters are not so simple. Because of what has happened I have taken revenge
on posterity." When I asked what he meant by the enigmatic phrase "taking revenge on posterity" he told me: "Today I have destroyed a new
arrangement of Nietzsche's *Will to Power* which contradicts the one made
by his sister Elisabeth Förster and on which I have worked for a long time."

The reason I set forth these memories only now, and did not do so during the time of the polemic against Heidegger started by Adorno and Löwith
("Philosopher in Needy Times") is that Szilasi, who was a close friend and
together with whom I had published the series *Überlieferung und Auftrag*
with Francke during his Swiss emigration, had continued to assert until
his death that we should never forget Heidegger's greatness as philosopher,
and that any argument with him should remain on the impersonal level
of philosophy. Only within this frame of reference could any personal considerations have meaning and foundation.

The problem of the tradition of Humanism which had come to the fore
during the historical situation in Germany described above became more
and more topical, not only as a purely theoretical but also as a political
problem. The theoretical and historical question was the question as to

my own intellectual identity. If—as already indicated—Heidegger's interpretation of Plato and Aristotle had meant the opening up of a new world for me and a new philosophical problematic, the question of the essence and the original structure of Humanism became all the more pressing precisely because Heidegger had negated its philosophical relevance on the basis of his view of the problem of Being as distinguished from that of being. External events forced me more and more to give prominence in my work to my problems with Humanism. The present essay is a continuation and, in a certain way, the conclusion of those efforts.

During the years 1938–39, I was commissioned to found the institute Studia Humanitatis under the patronage of the Royal Italian Academy in Berlin. The institute was to devote itself to the study of the history of Humanism and the Renaissance and their relation to antiquity. The realization of such a task under very difficult political circumstances owes much to the decisive initiative of Professor Enrico Castelli, then director of the Istituto di studi filosofici of the University of Rome.

In 1939 I moved, therefore, to Berlin; my associate professorship for the philosophy of Humanism and the Renaissance was also transferred to that university. The first decisive encounter in Berlin was a meeting with the publisher Küpper who had belonged to the circle around Stefan George and who had taken over the Bondi publishing house. He was a close friend of Kantorowitz, the author of the famous book on the Staufic emperor Frederick II, with whom Humanism starts in Sicily. I also met Riezler, who had originally been at the University of Frankfurt, and who had to resign from his office as Chancellor because of his Jewish wife, the daughter of the painter Max Liebermann. Among a number of other personalities was Guardini, who had also been prohibited by the National Socialists from lecturing and publishing. The foundation of my institute gave many the hope of finding help against the so-called "Germanic" ideology of the National Socialists. Thus, the problem of Humanism and of the Latin tradition found itself in a political situation which gave an unexpected topicality to scholarly research into Humanism.

After two years of preparation, the institute opened in Berlin on December 6, 1942. For the inaugural address I had won Professor Salvatore Riccobono, our leading specialist in Roman Law. He gave a lecture in Latin titled "On the Fate of Roman Law." Riccobono's Latin speech and its German translation were published by Küpper in the *Festschrift* to mark the opening of the institute. If, from an external point of view, the problem of Humanism had thus gained political prominence, where would the focus be for scholarly research into the problematic? In order to discuss this question, the publisher Küpper undertook to publish the *Jahrbuch der geistigen Überlieferung*, which I edited together with the two foremost classicists of their time, Otto and Reinhard. The aim of the contributions of Otto, Reinhard, and Friedrich was to treat the problematic of Humanism from different angles. My essay, "The Problem of the Beginning of Modern Thinking," my first still rather tentative outline of the problem of Humanism, developed following discussions with Otto. Only in the present book, which was stimulated to a large degree through the discussion and refutation of Heidegger's interpretation, can I try to evaluate the whole theoretical and historical problematic of Humanism.

It was only due to the efforts of Küpper and Enrico Castelli that we succeeded at that time in publishing in Italy two essays by Guardini in German: his "Death of Socrates" and "On Rainer Maria Rilke's Interpretation of Existence: An Interpretation of the *Duino Elegies* II, VIII, and IX." The German consul at Florence, Wolff—who had belonged to the George circle and who was made an Honorary Citizen of Florence after the war in gratitude for his efforts in saving the Ponte Vecchio from destruction— made it possible to introduce these publications into Germany. From among the translations of classical texts I would remind the reader of Reinhard's translation into German of Sophocles' *Antigone*. In the second volume of the *Jahrbuch der geistigen Überlieferung* (1942) I published for the first time Heidegger's "Plato's Teachings on Truth." It was prohibited to mention or to review it in the press; similarly, any separate publication of it was forbidden.

In the meantime, the political situation thrust itself more and more into the foreground. The publication of the third volume of the *Jahrbuch* was forbidden by the National Socialist authorities. The political situation in Italy—the collapse of the government, the Badoglio regime, the Republic of Salò—made any realization of the purely scholarly pursuits of the institute impossible, and so I resigned from my position.

A lectureship at the University of Zürich allowed me to bridge the time to the end of the war. Still, my most urgent problem was my argument with Heidegger about the nature of Humanism, which was as yet incomplete. Two months after the end of the war, through the good offices of the French and American occupation forces, Professor Castelli and I managed to visit Heidegger in his hut in the Black Forest. He handed me the manuscript of his "Letter on Humanism," which first appeared in the series *Überlieferung und Auftrag*, a series which I had earlier founded with my friend Szilasi in Switzerland, together with the publisher Francke. The "Letter" was published together with Heidegger's *Plato's Theory of Truth*, which I had already published in Germany.[7]

It was only Heidegger's fundamental clarification of his negative attitude toward Humanism—always in the context of the problem of the ontological difference—which made any further discussion of Humanism possible. I have subsequently developed my own position in my book *Potency of the Imagination* (*Macht der Phantasie*, 1979), in the two English language publications, *Rhetoric as Philosophy: The Humanist Tradition*, and especially *Heidegger and the Question of Renaissance Humanism*, as well as in the present essay.

The founding of the chair for the "Philosophy and Intellectual History of Humanism" twenty-five years ago at the University of Munich, the chair which I vacated as Professor Emeritus, and the foundation and direction of the *Humanistische Bibliothek* with the publisher Fink have been the practical results of my scholarly activities in the field of Humanistic Studies.

CHAPTER ONE

The Problem of the Word

1

Preamble: The Rejection of the Philosophical Significance of Humanism

THE FORMAL METHOD OF REASONING NOWADAYS ADOPTED BY PROPO-
nents of analytical philosophy and formal logic naturally brings with it a
negative attitude towards the traditions of Humanism. For according to
analytical philosophy, science is only applicable within the range of a system based, in each field, on its own particular premises, and of course
these premises cannot be proved because they form the system's own foundation. As a result, science can only be of a "formal" nature. There can
be no science outside the symbolic and formal range of a system. This
leads to the rejection not only of metaphysics, which claims to transcend
the limits of formal thought and language, but equally of all "Humanistic"
ways of thinking, including any attempts to apply poetic or rhetorical ideas
and devices, for instance, metaphors, wherever any of the science – and,
accordingly, philosophy – are concerned.

This negative attitude towards Humanism, which amounts to altogether
denying its philosophical impact, is not of recent date, but is deeply rooted in the entire rationalistic approach of modern thought. Descartes deliber-
ately banned all humanistic branches (philology, history, rhetoric and poetry)
from the realm of philosophy, stating that far from contributing to the clarity
of thought and speech, they tended to obscure it.[1] Moreover, Descartes

was convinced that there existed far more original minds outside the cir-
cles adhering to the Humanistic tradition than there were inside them,
identifying the latter with those who devoted themselves to the study of
letters (*litterae*): "Saepissime videamus illos, qui litteris operam nunquam
navarunt, longe solidius et clarius de obviis rebus judicare, quam qui perpetuo in scholis sunt versati."[2]

Thus, rhetoric—an art particularly important to the Humanists—was cen-
sured for acting on the passions of readers and listeners and distracting
them from the rigor of rational, deductive thought. Equally rejected was
any philosophical reasoning that depended on the validity of a factor such
as common sense (*sensus communis*), for the rigor of the rational process
alone could be considered as a true criterion for philosophy. The problem
"how" to formulate philosophical ideas does not even exist for Descartes:
the logical thought implicitly determines the style.

Throughout the evolution of philosophy after Descartes, this negative
judgment regarding the philosophical significance of Humanistic subjects
has, as a rule, remained unchanged. Hegel, the be-all and end-all of the
entire idealistic tradition, considered philosophy as "thinking contemplation," i.e., as a science aiming to grasp the essence of reality by means
of logical dialectical reasoning. Hegel's theoretical expositions determine
his judgment regarding the philosophical and historical significance of Humanism. The history of philosophy must serve to divest systems "of anything pertaining to their external features, their application to particular
cases, etc., that is, only the 'idea' itself must be shown in its logical
concept."[3]

Hegel accordingly criticizes Latin philosophy—which is extensively referred to by the Humanists—as a "popular" rather than a "speculative"
philosophy. He denies the thesis that the Roman evolution of law represents
a philosophical process. "The Roman world, which has killed living indi-
viduality in itself, has indeed produced formal patriotism and its virtue,
as well as an elaborate system of laws; but speculative philosophy could
not emerge from this death: good lawyers, the morality of a Tacitus."[4] In
this connection Cicero—one of the most crucial sources of Humanism—is
also brought into the picture: "Aristotelian philosophy was also called peripatetic philosophy, and this has become—for instance, in Cicero's times—a
kind of popular philosophy in which guise the profound, speculative method
of Aristotle was remodelled and made known."[5] Non-speculative
philosophy is not a "pure science," because it does not take cognition as

its direct starting-point. Hegel's criticism of Roman philosophy hence coincides with his rejection of common sense: the proponents of Ciceronian popular philosophy "cannot be considered as true philosophers, they represent common sense."[6]

Hegel accordingly assumes a radically negative attitude towards Humanism, for reasons that occur again and again since Descartes. Philosophy is exclusively recognized as a rational science which can only attain its appropriate form through reflection and through the "idea." In Hegel's opinion, Humanism does not do justice to an awareness of the idea, because it is too deeply involved with the world of fantasy and art; and for Hegel, as we know, art is merely an inadequate way of representing the idea. In art the idea is too closely connected with the concrete, the sensuous, so that it appears merely as an "ideal." "Too clumsy to represent thought as thought, Humanism resorts to the device of expressing itself in a sensuous form."[7]

Truth in Humanism is only amenable in a secondary, figurative way, it does not reveal itself as such, but "its source is . . . authority, the heart, the instincts, the inclinations, our natural being, a sense of justice . . . The content is the form, which is merely a natural one."[8] So for Hegel the Humanist philosophy belongs "to the superfluous phenomena that hardly yield much profit with regard to philosophy."[9]

We come across an equally negative attitude towards Cicero and his philosophical significance in the works of certain historians, Mommsen, for instance; and here, too, the background consists of a clearly rationalistic concept of philosophy. What Mommsen sees in Cicero's work is, above all, "the rise of the lawyer's speech as a genre of literature."[10] The only talent Mommsen granted Cicero was that of the stylist: "He was in fact such a thorough charlatan that it hardly mattered whose side he was on. A journalistic literature in the worst sense of the word, superabundant in words, as he himself admitted, but immeasurably poor in ideas; there was no subject on which he could not, with the aid of a few books, quickly whip up a readable essay by producing a translation or a commentary."[11]

Similar reasons are given by a scholar such as E. R. Curtius for his negative verdict on the Humanist philosophical tradition. When I was publishing a German translation of Garin's work on the philosophy of Humanism, the Romance scholar ridiculed the work and said that there was no justification whatsoever for publishing it, because the so-called philosophy of Humanism consisted of nothing but "exercises in rhetorical style."[12]

Ernst Cassirer maintains that even in those instances where Humanism unites philology and philosophy, "philosophy itself does not undergo a true methodical renewal."[13] In Humanism, philosophy seems "to develop merely a subordinate and limited efficacy."[14] Concerned with what he considered above all as philosophy—i.e., the problem of cognition—Cassirer only managed to find sparse traces of it in the Humanistic tradition. Even K. O. Apel states that the fight of the Humanists against the scholastic linguistic logic "was virtually fought without any philosophical equipment, almost exclusively by means of emotive protestations."[15] P. O. Kristeller, to whom we owe a detailed study of Ficino and many erudite historical investigations on Humanism, maintains that "Renaissance Humanism does not in itself represent a school or a compact system within philosophy, but is instead a cultural and educational program dealing essentially neither with classical philology nor with philosophy as such."[16] Jaeger also agrees that Humanism merely represents a particular concept of culture, based purely on the idea of human education and, in that sense, forming a renewed synthesis of the culture and education that was accepted by all nations of the Hellenocentric cultural world, i.e., the world of the Greeks and the way in which it was first typically exemplified by the Romans.[17]

This radical rejection of the philosophical significance of Humanism was also expressed by Heidegger in his "Letter on Humanism," which I first published in 1947. Heidegger also identifies Humanism with the affirmation of the "homo humanus" as a Roman ideal, an ideal ennobled through the adoption of the Greek concept of παιδεία. "In Rome we come across the first example of Humanism. It therefore remains in essence a specific Roman phenomenon, arising from the encounter of the Roman world with the culture of late Hellenism. The so-called Renaissance of the fourteenth and fifteenth centuries in Italy is a *renascentia romanitatis*."[18] Heidegger considers this type of Humanism as identical with that of the eighteenth century—as in Winkelmann, Goethe and Schiller—but he says that *it is not* the Humanism of Hölderling "because he conceives the destiny of mankind in a more pristine manner than the other 'Humanism' is capable of doing."[19]

Heidegger claims that the Humanistic approach does not grasp the essence of man: "In this sense the thought behind 'Being and Time' is against Humanism. . . . The thought is against Humanism because it underestimates the humanitas of man."[20] Heidegger's thesis is: If the term "Humanism" puts the accent on man as the starting point for philosophical reasoning—

hence, on an anthropological basis—then this precludes any original thinking from the very outset. We cannot, at this point, elaborate on the speculative grounds for Heidegger's attitude. But it is important to point out that his anti-Humanism evidently derives from the principle that validates the over-all traditional pattern of Humanism, i.e., as a movement that arrives at re-discovering the inherent values of mankind by way of literature, philology and rhetoric. It is precisely the anthropological affirmation of man—according to the traditional model outlined by Burckhardt—that leads to a humanistic thirst for glory, to the cult of the birthplaces of famous citizens, to a renewed interest in history and classical antiquity.

It is important to keep in mind these negative judgments on the philosophical significance of Humanism in the course of our further discussions.

2
"Verbum" and "Res" in Dante (1266–1321)

The most important theoretical premises of traditional philosophy which the Humanists had to tackle are actually contained in the following thesis in the first chapter of Dante's political work *De Monarchia:* "Since every non-original truth is always revealed on the basis of a first guiding truth, it is inevitable that every investigation should arrive at the cognition of this first truth and should refer to it analytically, in order to attain certainty about all the assertions that have their roots in it."[21]

Accordingly, the principal task of philosophical reasoning is the definition of being, and this can only be achieved through a rational process of thought. By way of the concept (χῶρος) and the definition (χωρισμός), rational thought claims to "grasp" the essence (οὐσία) of being. In this manner the meaning of being is once and for all "fixed" through the abstraction of time and place. All empirical variations—to which, by definition, no universality can be ascribed—are proved inessential. The only object of knowledge is that which "is," that which "lasts,"[22] that which "prevails forever and everywhere," that which is eternal (ἀίδιον) and immovable.[23] So beings in their truth are grasped by means of a rational process of deduction from the "original" and "first being."

For a tradition of this kind the problem of the intelligibility and rationality of beings (*res*) is of prime importance, as is clearly shown in the following formulation by Duns Scotus: "The soul is capable, by a purely rational process, to deal with the sciences, and that by keeping aloof from the noise of articulate speech."[24] Philosophical investigations must deal with the rational definition of beings, not with various historical forms of language, for "these do not concern the essence of things, but the laws of human speech."[25]

So the true and primary problem is the rational definition of beings (*res*), not that of the word (*verbum*). The word has to correspond to a rational and constant assessment of the "res," and that is why the essence of language is non-historical. For medieval philosophy – as summed up by Dante in his definition of the nature of knowledge – it is reason that determines the "res," and the "verbum" has to be proved by reason, which establishes its meaning once and for all. The human grasp of the "res" is consequently the starting point of traditional philosophy. It assumes that the "res" exist in and for themselves and are defined in their existence by reason, so that language must express the non-historical nature of beings. The verification of what is said (*verbum*) takes place with regard to a being which has been established rationally: ontology as a prerequisite for language.

Philosophy proceeds from the thing, not the word. Since beings are to be defined only through the rational process, the corresponding valid language can only be rational. That is, it is reason that lends the word its meaning. "Non sermoni res, sed rei sermo est subiectus."[26] It is the function of language to represent the expression of a rationally established meaning of beings. This tradition requires that the word should correspond to the nature of things. Language is tied to a non-historical concept of beings. Ontology as the foundation of language precludes any change or diversity in the meaning of words. The ontological definition of being with its inalterable meaning establishes "things" as existing "in themselves": "enuntiabilia nihil aliud esse, quam rationes aeternas rerum in mente divina."[27] Language is the expression of the eternal.

Dante's *De Monarchia*, in which he describes rational activity as the highest function of man, is based on this conception. The realization of this activity, which presupposes peace, is the task of the politician. "Satis igitur declaratum est quod *proprium opus humani generis* totaliter accepti est *actuare semper totam potentiam intellectus possibilis* . . . patet quod genus humanum in *quiete* sive *tranquillitate pacis* ad proprium suum opus . . . se habet."[28] This accounts for his theory of the universal monarch who, unlike the individual kings, rules the whole world, and whose task consists of preventing any alteration in the eternal order established and politically institutionalized by way of intellectual insight. In other words, it is the historical function of the universal monarch to see to it that no history will be made.

Dante also refers to the traditional theory of language which we have just discussed. In *De Vulgari Eloquentia* he stresses the need to affirm only that language which, in its universality and abstraction, avoids all local and temporal variations. He identifies this language with Latin: "Hence proceeded the inventors of the art of Latin. The Latin I speak of has as its property the inalterable *uniformity of the language of diverse times and places* [quedam inalterabilis locutionis *ydemptitas diversibus temporibus atque locis*]. As it was regulated through the concurrence of many nations, it is not subject to the arbitrariness of the individual and therefore *cannot be variable*. So it was invented in order to prevent us from being confused by the diversity of a language which fluctuates according to the will of individuals" [ne, propter variationem sermonis arbitrio singularium fluitantis].[29]

But simultaneously with his thesis about the need for a "grammatical" (as Dante called it), non-historical language, he also stresses the need for a *historical language.* In connection with his deliberations about his own functions as a poet and orator, he acclaims the language in which we live, love, and act in the realm of the "here" and "now," the language that differs in each country, thus reversing the premises of traditional philosophy.

As we have mentioned, traditional philosophy deals with the problem of the rational definition of beings, which proceeds from the "concipere mente simplici primo ens" and derives the "modo essendi" from this "conceptio" through the categories, in order to arrive at the determination of the "proprietas rei." Based on this ontological definition of beings, language in its philosophical function must not only be non-historical, it must also exclude all poetic and rhetorical elements because of their non-rational character.

The "orator," who is not concerned with the rational essence of things, but with their local and temporal implications, exercises an activity which, according to medieval speculation, belongs to the political or judicial realm. The orator deals with opinions, he aims at bringing his public over to his own side. Since rhetoric is not particularly concerned with the "logical aspect" of things, it may possibly obscure people's understanding of facts and is, in this respect, open to philosophical criticism such as Descartes'.

If rhetoric is acceptable, it is only in order to make theories more easily understandable, in which case it assumes a subordinate function, leading to popularizing science. Rhetoric and poetry use metaphors, but the logically appropriate word for each matter precludes the metaphorical reference as something lacking in precision: metaphor is logically "deficient," it is the expression of something "imprecise."

With his defense of the vernacular, Dante in effect reverses this conception. He abandons ontology as a prerequisite for language. In view of his function as a poet and political orator—and contrary to what he maintained in other passages of *De Vulgari Eloquentia* with regard to the poet's need for a non-historical language (i.e., Latin)—he praises the "historical" language. Through his poetry and rhetoric he aims at disclosing a world, the world of his own time and country, his own "here and now," a task which had never been acknowledged as the function of poetry in traditional medieval philosophy.

Above all, he affirms the fundamental function of the vernacular against the thesis of the prevalence of the universal, rational language: "It was this vernacular language of mine which unified my ancestors, for in it they spoke just like the fire that tempers the iron so that the smith can make a knife with it" [Questo mio volgare fu congiungitore deli miei generanti, che con esso parlavano, sí come'l fuoco è disponitore del ferro al fabbro che fa lo coltello].[30] The everyday language of "here" and "now"—*not* the logical, abstract, timeless language of eternity—is the "fire" with which man forges the instrument to create *his own* world. Elsewhere, to confirm his preference, Dante uses another image: "If a flame were to blaze up visibly from the window of a house and someone would ask whether there was a fire inside the building, and another would answer in the affirmative, I would not know whom to laugh at more. That is what my answer would sound like if I were to be asked whether I love my language."[31]

Is Dante's love, as a poet, for his own language—in contradistinction to the objective, "non-historical Latin language"—a subjective preference for the Florentine vernacular? Or does this statement have a more fundamental significance? The point, according to Dante, is the function of the poet to reveal the historical situation of a nation, and that is an important and fundamental task.

There are four principal functions that Dante ascribes to the poetic language, all four of which transcend the limits of a purely "literary," "aesthetic" function. First of all, its task is to "illuminate" reality and make it appear in its true significance: "Per hoc quoque quod illustre dicimus, intelligimus quid *illuminans* et *illuminatum* prefulgens."[32] Secondly, it is "cardinal," i.e., it forms the hinge on which the idiom of a nation rests and simultaneously moves.[33] Its third quality is that of being "aulica," that is, through its "illuminating" and "cardinal" functions, it creates the "aula" or the "court," as a homogeneous space for the community.[34] Since no such poetic language has as yet been created, Dante complains, "our language wanders around like a strange pilgrim and only finds shelter in lowly sanctuaries."[35] The fourth and last characteristic of the poetic language is its "curialitas."[36] "Curia" is the place where laws are established; the poetic language is the source from which we must draw in order to determine the rules of a nation's language.

There has been a tradition to reduce the scope of these statements by ascribing them to a purely "literary" domain, and thus denying them any philosophical significance. The reasons for this tradition are understandable: Dante's philosophy is rightly identified with scholasticism because of the speculative content of the *Divine Comedy*. But we must not forget that Dante, through his four fundamental qualifications of the poetic idiom, intended to disclose the historical range of his nation, irrespective of any rational traditional metaphysics or ontology. How are we to understand a mission of this kind? Let us remember that Dante claims this mission *for himself as a poet:* "And I confer this honor on that friend [i.e., the vernacular language] by making apparent what possible and hidden gifts he himself possesses through that which is his own achievement, namely, to reveal the devised message."[38]

The importance he attaches to a mission of this kind and to the corresponding human commitment comes out in the following dramatic sentences: "Over all those parts where it [the vernacular language] extends have I gone as a wanderer, almost begging [peregrino quasi mendicando sono andato] and have, against my own will, shown the wounds of fortune [la piaga della fortuna] that are often unjustly held against the wounded. Indeed I was a ship without sails and without a rudder, swept to diverse ports and estuaries and shores by the dry wind that evokes painful poverty" [Veramente io sono stato legno sanza vela e sanza governo, portato a diversi porti e focie liti dal vento secco che vapora la dolorosa povertade].[39]

The philosophical question that suggests itself here is: which language is the crucial one? Is it the rational language deriving from the problem of being, that is, from an ontology, in order to define the genus and species of things? With Dante, who had followed the existing tradition in his *De Monarchia* by defining philosophy as a study of the problem of beings and its logical truth, the leading function of the poetic idiom moves into the foreground, as shown in these crucial statements. Here he proceeds from the poetic, rather than the rational, language. Does this departure represent a shift from the traditional to a new humanistic philosophy? Let us keep in mind that to proceed from the problem of being, i.e., from an ontology, means to uphold the thesis of the universality of language, that is, its independence from local or temporal circumstances. But does not Dante's "new" approach imply that the meaning of beings is never the same, that things acquire a new meaning in each concrete historical situation, so that the prevalence of rational thought and language proves a fallacy? Does this problem perhaps arise from the difficulties of the traditional medieval assertion that the individual case is "ineffable?"

Dante's argument about the "historical" (*volgare*) and poetic language has no foundation in the traditional ontology. This would have prevented his affirmation of the manifold meanings of the word and of its historical function, as well as his recognition of the task of a metaphorical language in various historical situations. Dante's thesis about the four functions of poetry deserves to be attributed a fundamental theoretical significance: poetry has an illuminating function; it creates the "aula" or court as the place for a community and, at the same time, the "curia" or tribunal where the rules of the language are set.

The awareness of a difference between the traditional conception of a "universal" language that has to be of a non-historical character and a language that forges ahead in its ever-changing, historical nature points to an entirely new set of problems in the relationship between "res" and "verba." Dante's interpreters have laid little or no stress on the surprising discrepancy between his opposing statements in *De Vulgari Eloquentia* and *Convivio,* and have thus covered up the problems it raises. The present work is meant to raise and answer these questions. I intend to show that the radical difference between the antique-medieval and the "new" humanistic philosophies lies in the fact that the former proceeds from an ontology, a theory of beings, while the specific Humanistic process of thought begins with the problem of words, above all the poetic idiom. We shall find out what conclusions this difference allows us to draw from a philosophical point of view.

The radical difference of rational and poetic language seems to be an essential part of Western thought. Plato, in his interpretation of Socrates, takes great pains to emphasize the rational "idea" as an essential factor in the definition of being: language as an expression of the episteme. Yet in his *Phaedrus*,[40] where Socrates reclines on the banks of the Ilyssos and listens to the sound of the cicadas, he says that they are the descendants of those men who were so enraptured by the songs of the Muses that they forgot everything else, including food. It is with the song of the Muses—not with rational thinking—that something tremendous happens. Here Plato seems to forget the priority of the "episteme."

3

Poetry as Theology, as "Altera Philosophia": Albertino Mussato (1261–1329)

Albertino Mussato, a contemporary of Dante, belonged to the circle of Italian poets known as the "cenacolo Padovano." Like a number of Humanists, he was a statesman, an historian, and a Latin poet. He was crowned poet laureate in Padua in 1315, in recognition of his tragedy *Ecerinis*, which dramatizes the life of the tyrant Ezzelino da Romano. He affirms the primal function of the poetic idiom, and with this affirmation he, too, abandons the theory of the ontological foundation of language. Mussato's letters[41] about the nature of poetry belong to the most significant early Humanistic texts on the subject. According to Mussato, it is the language of poetry that discloses and "illuminates" the historicity of man.

Poetry does not deal with absolute truth, it is constantly concerned with revealing the historical world, which includes the prevailing gods and institutions of each era. The poet's function is to make apparent the significance of the past in so far as it has a decisive effect of the future. The origin should not be sought in entities, which come into being, exist and vanish; it is only revealed in and through poetry by the impact of words. Mussato goes so far as to make the bold claim that he as a poet existed before the warriors he celebrates in his poem, for it is through his work that the heroes with their glorious exploits emerge from obscurity: "It is *I* who reclaimed Pergamon, the citadel of the Dardanian Teucrian; before the Dardanian arrived in Troy, *I was there*."[42]

The language of poetry does not hark back to an ontological background. The contrast between the traditional medieval attitude and that of Mussato may be illustrated by two antipodal interpretations of the laurel wreath, the symbol of the poet's distinction. From the traditional viewpoint, the essential function of poetry was to express the ontologically established truth. For Mussato, however, it represented the original and eternal manifestation of divine power, such as it is revealed in history, where things are constantly re-discovered and assume a new significance. "And as the laurel is always green and is never picked with withered leaves, so poetry possesses that eternal beauty. That is why the foreheads of seers are crowned with laurels."[43] Poetry, as symbolized by the ever-green foliage of the laurel, assumes the function of original revelation.

The opposite view, entirely corresponding with the traditional ontological approach, is voiced by a contemporary critic of Mussato's, a monk of the preaching order whom we know as Fra Giovannino of Mantua. For him the crucial factor is the true meaning of beings as defined and firmly established through the rational process. Mussato's quest for the ever-changing historical significance of beings is not acknowledged by the preacher as a philosophical problem. It is invalidated by his conception of beings as a foundation for languages. As a result, he interprets the circular laurel wreath, the symbol of poetry, as something that keeps away from the center—i.e., the center of gravity, which he identifies with truth—so that it is "external" and "untenable." "The wreath is made of laurel, which externally has the green color and the scent; but internally it contains bitterness through its fruit, which is very bitter. So poetry externally possesses a certain beauty in its words, but internally it has the bitterness of vanity."[44]

Mussato's thesis about the original function of poetry leads to his idea of its sacral, divine nature. He explicitly maintains that poetry is an "ars divina" and, in fact, a "theology of the world."[45] He passionately reproaches those who do not acknowledge the outstanding sacral role of poetry with neglecting its high "ministerium."[46]

Through the divine spirit manifesting itself in the language of poetry, all beings—i.e., things, men, institutions, the gods of different periods— are disclosed by the rhythmic, regulated, and at the same time regulating, language of poetry. The divine spirit—and this is emphasized by Mussato— again and again reveals and conceals itself in the varying forms of the gods and institutions of various periods. In this connection, our author sees a parallelism in the manifestations of classical antiquity and those of the Old Testament. In antique religion Jupiter struck the Titans with lightning. In the Old Testament God strikes mankind with the confusion of languages: "confundit linguas Deus hic, qui fulmina jecit, qui Deus est nobis, Jupiter ille fuit."[47] In the Greek religion the poets said of the gods that they made their vows at the Styx. Here Mussato sees a correspondence with Christ's words that the water of baptism is the source of life: "in unda baptismi nostrae numen consistere vitae."[48]

Against Mussato's statement that poetry is a "theologia mundi," a "prima philosophia"—which upsets the medieval conception of the relationship between theology and poetry—Giovannino of Mantua argued that Mussato had written obscene Priapic poems when he was young. Mussato answered that this was no argument against his thesis. Poetry possesses the attribute of being a "theologia mundi," not because its statements are identical with a particular conception of the divine in a particular historical period, but it is divine because beings are revealed in it from their historical aspects. As for the preacher's objection against obscenity, Mussato replied that it, too, belonged to the manifestations of being: "Sometimes I talk about the appearances of holy Minerva, and Venus is also a welcome adjunct to my functions."[49]

It is through poetry that the origins speak and reveal themselves, though they also veil themselves in each of the different images [sub cortice figuris]. Every work of poetry that today brings beings to our mind for our contemplation has at one time been theology,[50] and it is therefore the poet who bears God in his heart and on his tongue.[51]

4

Petrarch (1304–1374) and His Unsuccessful Theoretical Defense of Poetry

We must remember what difficulties Humanism had to face in confronting traditional Christian metaphysics. According to medieval philosophy, which was an ontology based on the classical metaphysics of Plato and Aristotle, the rationally established theory of beings was the foundation of words, of language. Poetry and rhetoric had no philosophical function or sig-

nificance unless they corresponded with a theory of beings established
by the ontologists. Thus poetry could only be legitimately acknowledged
as an aid, for instance, to theology. This was the natural and necessary
result of the conception of philosophy as a rational process towards the
definition of beings. Poetry is either a metaphorical expression of truth,
or else it is pure falsehood, individual fancy, a fairy-tale for amusement.
When Humanists like Dante and Mussato renounced the problem of being and proceeded instead to invest the poetic idiom with the function of
original revelation, this put a stop to the entire traditional way of thinking
and started off a new process of thought.

So far we have not attempted to provide a theoretical justification for
our above thesis. Before we do so, it is useful to show some concrete examples of the main difficulties the Humanists had to cope with in view of
the ontological roots of the Christian tradition. We must not forget that
Horace, for example, in his epistle to the Pisones, affirmed the "illuminating" function of poetry. Did the Humanists in fact give reasons for this thesis?

After Dante and Mussato, it was Petrarch's turn to experience the great
dilemma of this new departure in the field of poetry, and to express the
contradictions that resulted because of the existing tradition. As already
pointed out, traditional philosophy had maintained that reason defines beings and that the word is "measured" by reason. The fundamental problem, accordingly, is the rational definition of entities, not the word. The
rationality of the subject determines the precision of the meaning of a word.
For Aristotle the categories were the instruments with which to define entities as entities (τὰ ὄντα),[52] and their original Greek meaning of "accusation" (in the sense of testifying something about something) points to
the fact that their predicative, logical character is an essential part of the
judgment and of the statement: where reason prevails, it does not matter
by whom or where or when something is said, it only matters *what* is said.
The thing in itself is what matters. The metaphorical expression is a renun-
ciation of logical "stringency" and therefore of "science." What function,
then, can the metaphorical language of poetry perform?

Petrarch, who still belongs to this ontological metaphysical tradition and
yet experiences the impact of words in metaphors, is confronted with fundamental difficulties. When he uses the images "alloro" (laurel), "lauro" (a
synonym for laurel), "l'aura" (the rustling wind), "l'auro" (the golden) and
"Laura" (the name of his beloved) in his collection of poems (*Canzoniere*),
he is faced with the question whether he is hereby revealing a reality that

is unattainable through logical speech, or whether he is expressing a pure fiction. Does not his insight in establishing a correspondence between the name of a woman and a plant open up a reality that could never become visible in the realm of reason, i.e., in a realm beyond time and place?

In the *Canzoniere* Petrarch makes a crucial avowal:

> Di me non pianger, tu chè miei dì fersi
> morendo eterni, e nel'interno lume,
> quando mostrai de chiuder, gli occhi apersi.
>   (CCLXXIX)

> Do not weep for me, for my days, though mortal,
> Will be eternal, in the inner light
> I seemed to shut my eyes, but opened them.

Is this meant as a mere "literary" game? In his oration at the Capitol in Rome in 1344, when he was crowned poet laureate, he explicitly stated that the poet can only create through the inner power that God had implanted in man: ". . . in qua nihil agitur sine interna quadam et divinitus in animum vatis infusa vi."[53] Referring to Cicero's speech "Pro Archia" in this solemn oration, Petrarch maintains that the poet, because of his divine faculty, deserves to be called "holy": "jure sanctos appellat poetas." In his epistle to Zoilo he says: "To be insane, I admit, is proper to the stimulated mind" [Insanire licet, fateor, mens concitata]: through insanity man can transcend his workaday life,[54] and our poet ends with the radical statement: "There can be no ingenuity without a dash of madness."[55]

Are we dealing here with the originality of poetic, imaginative metaphorical language, or with purely subjective talent? "The human tongue would have remained dumb, so to speak, had the muses been absent from the universal spirit."[56] But if it is the function of philosophy to determine the universal meaning of words, irrespective of time and place and by means of the rational process, then what can be the significance of poetry? Every language has to be "true" in order to be valid, but poetic images are "logically" untrue. So what function is there for poetry to fulfil?

This is the question Petrarch asks himself in his poem *Africa*. What is poetic license? How does it relate to truth? "Non illa licentia vatum est quam multis placuisse palam est."[57] His speech at the Capitol begins with the same question: "It is appropriate, honored gentlemen, to know the function and profession [of the poet] for most, if not all, people follow mere opinions in this respect."[58] In his poem *Africa* the answer is: "It is, therefore, appropriate that everything written by the poet be anchored in the securest foundation of truth."[59] He condemns those poets who do not follow this principle: "He who merely invents everything he says deserves neither the calling of a poet nor the dignity of a prophet, but the name of liar."[60]

We have as yet failed to answer the question why there is any need for fiction in addition to philosophical truth, a question that was raised again and again in the medieval tradition. Petrarch's answer is: Poetry hides truth under a veil (*velamen*): "sub velamine figmentorum, nunc fisica, nunc moralia, nunc hystorias comprehendisse."[61] In the poem *Africa* it is a cloud, rather than a veil: "amena at varia sub nube potest abscondere se se."[62] But why should things be hidden, rather than clearly and distinctly said? The answers provided by Petrarch are characteristic, either because they show that he wanted to defend poetry at all costs, or because they speak of his difficult position in view of the prevailing tradition of a rationally established ontology.

In his letter to Zoilo the solution to the problem sounds rather lamentable: "The metaphor, the poetic veil, is necessary lest the sharpness of truth should injure the eye; it is the nubes that mitigate the appearance of an object and hence attract the observer."[63] Similarly, he says in the *Oratio* that poetry "has a sweeter effect [dulcior fit poesis] the more laboriously the truth is sought [quo laboriosius quesita veritas]; once it is discovered, it is more and more enjoyable [magis atque magis inventa dulcescit]."[64] In *Africa* he says that the poets, through their art of concealing, "provide the reader with the great pleasure of deciphering their work."[65]

The profound significance the Humanists attached to the question concerning the role of poetry can be confirmed by a reference to Boccaccio's *De natura deorum*. Boccaccio repeatedly points out that the Scriptures contain metaphors and other poetic expressions, so poetry must have had an original, sacral function. He refers to the Old Testament, where Moses speaks of God as a burning bush: "The spirit showed a burning bush, in which Moses saw a blazing flame."[66] Elsewhere he writes about the New Testament: "The Holy Scripture is nothing but a poetic fiction when it says that Christ is a lion, a lamb or a worm, and then a dragon . . . . How do the words of the Saviour sound in the Gospels if not like a speech with a strange meaning, a manner of speech that we call by the common name of allegory?" In the following sentence he arrives at the conclusion: "not only is poetry theology, theology is also poetry."[67]

In the *Genealogia deorum* Boccaccio also alludes to the theory that poetry throws a veil over things. "When the veil or the rind is taken off poetry, the intention of the story-teller manifests itself [cuius amoto cortice, patet intentio fabulantis]. So if anything stimulating appears under the fabulous veil, the story has not been useless."[68]

Boccaccio repeats the saying that the poetic tale "springs from the heart of God" [ex sinu Dei procedens], that the excitement it causes is as sublime as the soul's urge to speak,[69] and that it has an "inventive" character [fervor . . . exquisite inveniendi]. "So to cut my speech short, what I have said already proves that the poetic faculty is a property of pious men [satis apparere potest piis hominibus poesim facultatem esse] and that they draw their origin from the realm of the divine and receive their fame from the effect."[70]

Poetry as theology or as literary fiction? Is it the function of the logical or the metaphorical language to disclose the meaning of beings? Is ontology a prerequisite for philology or the reverse?

CHAPTER TWO

The Appeal and the Word

1
Philology as "Tropology":
Leonardo Bruni (1370–1444)

TRADITIONAL PHILOSOPHY STARTS FROM THE PROBLEM OF BEING: ITS rational determination forms the starting point for a discussion of the meaning of the word. The problem of the poetic word and its function highlight an important question: is it possible to discover a "new" philosophizing in the humanist tradition on the basis of the problematic of the word? We have already pointed to the difficulties which confronted the humanists whose roots lay in traditional thought.

On the basis of what experience is it possible, indeed necessary, to start from the problematic of the word in order to begin a new kind of philosophy that does not arise from the problematic of being? And to what new understanding of the philosophy of beings does this problematic lead in its turn?

If we want to tackle this task, we must return to the work of the humanist Leonardo Bruni. As he complains in his book *Ad P. P. Histrum Dialogus*, the situation of science in his time demands a completely new relationship to the classical tradition. In the present time it is important to regain the essential meaning of the classical text: "Equidem fateor non tam cupide Orpheum (ut poetae tradunt) Eurydicis amore infernas adisse sedes, quam ego, si spes modo aliqua offeratur antiquos illos praestantes viros intuendi, ad ultimas pentrarim terras."[1]

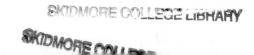

As a concrete task, he undertakes making a new translation of the *Nico-machean Ethics* and pitting it against the *Liber ethicorum* of Robert Gros-seteste (written 1247) and the translation of Wilhelm of Moerbeke. Bruni accomplishes his work in the years 1416–17. It is only in the frame of such a task that we are able to show in exemplary manner how (i.e., out of which experiences) the problem of the word steps into the foreground of philosophy, thus achieving a complete reversal of traditional philosophiz-ing, which then forms the essence of the specific way of humanist thinking.

For scholastic thought, the object, the "being" in its rational essence, treated in the text was the basic measure for judging the translation of a philosophical treatise; the determination of the "subject matter" has to be anchored in a rational justification. In *De divisione naturae* Scotus Eriu-gena emphasizes that it is impossible to gain true knowledge without any rational justification. The meaning of an expression transcends its histori-cal changeability. The rationally defined "res" as the starting point of philosophy determines the discourse, and not vice versa. "Scientia" can in no way take into consideration the historic, singular situation of language.

The radical difference between the medieval and the new starting point lies in the fact that the former begins with the question of being while the latter starts with the question of the word. An exemplary instance of this difference can be seen in the criticism levelled against Bruni's translation by Alfonso Garcia de Cartagena (1384–1456). Cartagena admonishes the reader to start in the traditional mode from the purely scientific and ra-tional definition of being [sub restrictis et proprissimis verbis, qua scien-tifica sunt discutere].[2] A translation has to respect the simplicity of being, viz., the exclusively precise and logical significance of the "res," which means that any poetic or rhetorical rendering must be deemed unessential.

It is significant for our problem that of all people Marsilio Ficino—the best known representative of traditional platonizing metaphysics among the humanists—calls Cartagena "summus metaphysicus": one more proof of how Ficino's Platonism does not admit any understanding of the "new" philosophy out of the experience of the word.

We do not mention Cartagena here in order to quote a critical contempo-rary of Bruni, but because we find in this Spanish author precisely the conditions set by rational philosophy for the traditional theory of translation.

In Bruni we do not find ontology, or logic as the foundation of language. This would prevent right from the beginning the experience of the manifold and the changing meaning of the words from which the humanists take their start. When confronting linguistic problems Bruni never starts from a prior rational definition in order to determine the meaning of the words. Nor is it essential for Bruni—as some critics maintain—that this new problematic of the word pertain to man and that we move therefore into the realm of subjectivity; rather, the problematic lies in a novel understanding of objectivity whose essence and structure must be discovered by us. In order to view the full problematic which Bruni reveals, we need to remind ourselves of some sentences in Cicero's *De oratore* which are in effect the precondition and the starting point of the humanistic experience and of humanistic thought: "There is nothing in the nature of things whose word or name we could not apply to other things. But because we can extract something similar from everything, light is shed on a speech through a single word which has a similtude."[3] Thus the essence of the word is a "translatum," a "tropus"; but does, therefore, the love of the word, philology, prove to be a "tropology?"

The reference to the rational determination of the "res" is the point of departure of traditional philosophy and it presupposes that the "res" exists per se and that it can be recognized in its existence through "ratio," and thus expressed in language. But when Bruni recognizes that the same expression acquires different meanings *in different contexts*, he is forced to admit that words have no rigidity which results from any rational determination, rather they have a "mollitia" which is essential to them: "Verba autem ipsa inter se quam molliter componenda et coagmentanda sunt eorumque continuatio et quasi textura omnis aurium sensu, . . . moderanda."[4] Bruni no longer attributes meaning to being through rational determination; he does this through the context within which the word stands in a work. This *context* with which the philologue is confronted is the original horizon in which a word receives its different meanings and can, therefore, be used variably: "*usus* ergo, qui tunc dominus fuit, etiam hodie dominus est . . . Nos vero haec omnia variamus *usu* iubente."[5] Neither in translation nor in everyday life does "logical" significance have preeminence.

For Bruni the subjectivity of man is never the basis in which the meaning of the word is rooted—this understanding would only confirm the traditional interpretation of Humanism as an anthropology—but rather the basis is the *context* with which the philologist has to deal, just as in everyday life human beings transfer different meanings to the same word in the "context" of different situations. The word "red" has a different meaning in the framework of experimental physics, political situations or traffic regulations. The proper meaning of language is verifiable only in the frame of a context (for philologists as for any other human being), within the frame of the situation, and not on the basis of the rational determination of the "res."

Bruni talks of the richness and the abundance of all that imposes upon us life [ubertatem et abundantiam rerum ad vitam pertinentium];[6] and he draws attention to the speed and agility which has to be exercised in life;[7] such statements are only possible on the basis of the experience that the needs which manifest themselves in various contexts and situations are the source of precise language, and never the purely abstract and rational determination of words. Speed and agility [celeritas et agilitas] are necessary where we have to respond always differently, i.e., "here" and "now" to the appeal of reality which makes itself known in the context or situation of experienced life. If we – like many critics of Bruni's work – emphasize only the "varietas" which he stresses, and forget that this "varietas" can be recognized only in the frame of the varying appeals of life situations, then we completely overlook his point of departure and the import of a philosophy which results from the problematic of the word.

The novelty of Bruni's thinking with regard to the "connexio," the connection of words, is precisely the understanding that it is not the rational "connexio" which matters, but rather its changeability in every "context" and in every "situation." An experience and the related understanding of it become possible only when the meaning of the "res" is investigated and determined in its *historicity*.

It is not the positing of the accidental, the variable in place of an abstract essence which is, as is frequently maintained, the "new" in Bruni's thought; rather, it is that he raises the problem of the word as answer to the challenge which life continually imposes in time and space. In this original system of relationships rests our "humanitas" and the original and genuine – not abstract – philosophy: "cuius ex fontibus haec omnis nostra derivatur humanitas."[8]

If the problem of philosophy is no longer understood as the rational determination of being, but as the response to the existential appeal which happens when interpreting the signifying word, then philosophy no longer begins with the category of the "truth" of being, but with the individual "unhiddenness" of being in its historical situation. Therefore, Bruni maintains, it is necessary not to withdraw into isolation but to gain reality through one's own language in and out of given situations: not in rational, but in

rhetorical language [Etenim absurdum est intra parietes atque in solitu-
dine secum loqui, multaque agitare, in oculis autem hominum atque in
coetu veluti nihi sapias obmutescere].[9]

If therefore a critic of Bruni's work maintains that Bruni has detached
the "res" from its ontological foundation, and that the immutable definition has been replaced by the variability of the "res," that critic has over-
looked the essential aspect of the question, namely, in which sphere the
mentioned variability is rooted. Only when we take recourse to this fundamental problem does it become possible to maintain that the historical
reality is indeed essential, in contrast to the Aristotelian thesis that only
the rationally determined οὐσία is the essence and that therefore all spa-
tial and temporal relations are purely accidental. The significance of words
springs neither from the source of human subjectivity nor from the relativity of beings, but from the individually variable appeals which humans
have to face in different situations. In this way Bruni liberates the problem
of language from abstract and purely theoretical discussions.

For Bruni "ingenium" and not "ratio" is the last resort when we have
to respond to the appeal which arises out of individual and variable situations. Versatility, "agility," "versutia" belong essentially to the "ingenium,"
while the "ratio" is essentially "rigid." Rigidity results from the rational
determination of beings, while the "versutia" arises because language has
to be versatile or "agile" in responding to the situation and to the context
of the work: "ingenium . . . versutiusque reddit."[10] Through its own "acumen," the "ingenium" discovers relationships and similarities, "similitudines."[11] This is why the "ingenium" is as fast as lightning.[12]

Logic is the science of the exact and justifying language, but not a "rich"
language. Tropes and metaphors, the "dicendi figura," are versatile and
copious forms of linguistic expressions found in the framework of the "here"
and "now." These are the characteristics of "ingenious" speech: "facundia
et dicendi figura ingenium . . . praeclare instituere atque alere potest."[13]
[(Ingenium) necesse sit, ut *momento temporis ad rem se applicet*].[14]

The ever-changing system of coordinates for the significance of words
reveals itself in the form of challenges in historical situations; they create
the sphere in which the activity of the "ingenium" first obtains its function. If, however, some critics of Bruni emphasize that the attribution of
meaning to words follows as a result of men's subjectivity, then they miss
the central point of the new thinking of humanism. Whereas in the traditional "Scientia rerum" the meaning of the word is verified by reference

to being and by the way it is rationally determined, Bruni examines the word in the light of the varying contexts and situations with a view to the appeals which face human existence; in fact, it is exactly this which constitutes the activity of the "ingenium": "Volo igitur huic ingenio,. . . ardentissimam cupiditatem inesse discendi, ita ut nullum genus disciplinae aspernetur, nullum a se alienum existimet."[15]

A "rich" language, a "copia verborum" — one in which every word receives a new meaning in each new context — is required, and can be grasped only when we understand the following: first, why the word is recognized as the response to claims made on humans, out of which response arises the meaning of being; second, why the problem of the word takes the foreground in lieu of being; and third, why the ingenium is the basic faculty which discovers relationships or which separates that which has already been linked together.

Out of these considerations arises the question: what is the meaning of Bruni's thesis that the "scientia rerum" is obscure and abstract as long as it is not enlightened by the splendor of the "litterae": "Scientia rerum quamvis ingens, si splendore careat litterarum, abdita quaedam obscuraque videtur?"[16] The "scientia rerum" deals with the problem of beings, and its rationally fixed determinants; the "litterae," however, start from the experience of the changing meanings of words. If this fact is not experienced, language not only remains rigid and immovable, but it also ignores the historicity of the word. This is the meaning of Bruni's words: "Ego nequeo satis mirari, quo pacto philosophiam didicerint, cum literas ignorent."[17]

When Bruni speaks of "rozzi e grossi e senza perizia di lettere, dotti . . . al modo fratesco scolastico,"[18] we should not take this criticism of the scholastics to indicate incompetence in a particular discipline; rather he is referring to something much more fundamental: ignorance of the "litterae" is ignorance of the philosophy out of which arises the problem of the word. Without a consciousness of this problem, one overlooks the historicity of the word: "Imperita . . . verborum omnia in hac temporum nostrorum faece confudit."[19] A knowledge of the "litterae" coincides with the experience of the changeable meaning of reality. Whoever has not made this experience through philology, and afterwards in life through the claims made by the historic situation, fails to interpret correctly the appeals in which every human finds himself: "nec verba nec significata intelligunt."[20] This is also the meaning of the "magnam et tritam et accuratam et reconditam litterarum peritiam,"[21] through which we humans first "nulla in re vacui rudesque videamur."[22] In this sense, Bruni makes a claim for a "vera philosophia, veraque scientia no fatua."[23] Elsewhere we read: ". . . neque contemplativa propria est hominis vita, sed activa. *Non enim, qua homo est, contemplatur.* . . . Justitiam vero, ac temperantiam et fortitudinem, ceterasque morales virtutes *exercet ut homo.*"[24] Dante's theses on the essence and function of poetry, which take their departure from an affirmation of the historical word, gain their importance in light of the recognition that language acquires its meaning only within the claims of a determinate time and a determinate location.

I shall conclude this section with a remark on the necessary and correct interpretation of the concept "ornatus," which for Bruni is an essential element in original language. "Ornatus" has the same meaning as the Greek κόσμος in the sense that it refers to a unity of a complex whole which results from relationships.[25] If we start from the problem of the rationally determined beings, we arrive necessarily at "ornatus" as a static togetherness of parts; however, if we start instead from the problem of the appeal in which humans find themselves and to which they respond through the word in varying situations, then the "ornatus" of rhetorical language is the form of original language as realized in the "here" and "now": "Iam vero illa verborum sententiarumque ornamenta, quae tamquam stellae quaedam et faces orationem illuminant et admirabilem reddunt, instrumenta oratorum propria sunt."[26]

2

The "Lamia" of Angelo Poliziano (1454–1494):
A "Literary" Fable?

The following problem emerges out of the foregoing discussion: what does a humanist mean by "philosopher?" Does he refer to a metaphysician, or to a philologist, an expounder of texts, an "interpres?" If, furthermore, the humanist no longer uses the rational metaphysical tractatus, which new form of expression will he choose? Can we take the metaphoric way of expression to be a form of philosophy? But in what way will this mode of discourse differ from the "literary metaphor," i.e., from the fable? In order to give a preliminary answer to these questions, we must go back to Poliziano's "Lamia."

"Lamia"—the "witch"—is the title of Poliziano's inaugural lecture, which he held in the Studio at Florence as the introduction to his interpretation of Aristotles's *Analytica Priora.* The theme of this lecture is a double one: a clarification of the traditional concept of philosophy and a discussion of whether Poliziano himself can be called a philosopher according to the traditional model of ontological metaphysicians. His lecture is marked by the use of two metaphorical tales, and so it had predominantly been taken to be a literary work. The first tale—a report on the old women who congregate at the well "fonte lucente" next to Poliziano's house near Fiesole—concerns some old witches who talk critically about Poliziano's activities while on their way to Florence. The second metaphorical tale at the end of the lecture refers to an owl—the symbol of philosophy—who admonishes other birds not to make their nests in a certain tree because they run the risk of becoming entangled in mistletoe.

What do these metaphors mean? What do they signify? Is this all only a literary game? Why does Poliziano frame the discussion of two such important problems as the definition of the essence of philosophy and the clarification of his own activities by two metaphorical tales?

The text underlines the fact that fairy tales (*fabulae*) not only have a "literary" character, but are also *tools of philosophy:* "Fabellae . . . non rudimentum sed et instrumentum quandoque philosophiae sunt."[27] In order to stress their speculative character, our author identifies "fable" with "myth," referring to Aristotle, who defines the philosopher as a "philomythos," the lover of myths: ". . . ut Aristoteles ait, etiam philosophus natura *philomythos, idest fabulae studiosus est.*"[28]

Later on we will see the importance of metaphors for the humanists: Vives uses them in his *Fabula de homine,* Erasmus in his *Praise of Folly,* L. B. Alberti in his *Momus.* But it is already important at this point to bring up the problem of the essence of metaphor in order to decide whether there is a difference between the "literary metaphor" in the form of a "fable" and the μῦθος as a philosophical metaphor. Only on the basis of this differentiation will it be possible to decide whether "Lamia" has a predominantly "literary" or "philosophical" character.

We must first understand that within the rationalistic tradition of modern thinking the metaphor has not only been denied any speculative function, but has even been regarded as an expression of the inability to rise to the height of the concept. Its "imaginative" character provides only the material for an intellectual assessment. Rational thinking, by its own processes, deepens the perception of what is common to several things in order then to liberate itself from their superficiality and relativity.[29] Rational cognition surpasses the metaphor inasmuch as the metaphor remains attached to the superficiality of the image.[30]

But let us return to the Latin tradition. Quintilian defines allegoric speech as a string of metaphors: "allegorian facit continua metaphora,"[31] i.e., a string of "translations." And rhetoric defines the "tropus" as an "exchange" of words "verborum immutatio,"[32] or as the "verbum translatum."[33] One word is put in the place of another, "proper" word (*verbum proprium*): lion in lieu of Achilles. Even the word μεταφορά, from μεταφέρειν, to "translate," is itself a tropus. Let us keep in mind that μεταφέρειν originally denotes as expression which does not arise within the realm of philology: it denotes a concrete action, in fact, the translation of an object from one place to another.[34] We should, therefore, not forget that in the area of philology a translation is only possible when a "transition," a "bridge," has been found, something in common which "connects" one place with another. Only much later does the expression μεταφορά appear in the field of philology, when it becomes a "metaphor" itself.

From its own standpoint, logic defines the "tropus," the metaphor, as an "improper" expression: the replacement of the meaning of one word by another is possible only on the basis of the "rational impropriety" of that expression. Irony, which Poliziano uses constantly, is a "tropus," too, insofar as the "proper" or "exact" word is replaced by an antonym (Tersites as lion), but in such a fashion that in the same discourse the falseness of the inversion becomes visible: ". . . quo contraria ostenduntur, ironeia est."[35] In any case, the tropus, the metaphor and the allegory presuppose the "ingenious" activity of the mind.[36] A translation of expressions is only possible if previously existing "similitudines," "similarities," between the translated terms have been found (*invenire*): the "similarity" is the "bridge" which makes the translation possible.

Traditionally, the "tropus" has been assigned the function of an ornament of speech in order to overcome boredom (*taedium*) and to induce "delight" (*delectatione*).[37] A purely rational discourse develops on the basis of an already "found" premise, from which the consequences are deduced: such a discourse does not need any "ornament" because it is conducted rationally and without "ingenium."

Here we face our first problem: what do we understand by the "verbum proprium?" Traditionally, it is that which has been "fixed" by logic
in its universal but abstract meaning. We have already pointed out that
the "being-there" is continuously placed in (and is indeed confronted with)
differing and new situations, and is therefore forced to refer to "tropes."
We gave the example of how the expression "red," which in optics is given
its general scientific meaning, is constantly given new and differing meanings: in the sign system of traffic, in the realm of politics, or, in the area
of human relationships, as an expression of a passion, perhaps signified
by a red rose. In these different situations the scientific definition of the
word "red" is evidently "improper." The "propriety" of the expression reveals
its narrowness when it is identified only with its rational determination.

Can we therefore assume from the foregoing that poetic language which
uses metaphor has, as Dante and Mussato maintain, priority and a philosophical function?

The problem arising from Poliziano's thesis about the importance of
the metaphoric fable as myth is the distinction between the "literary fable" and the philosophical metaphor or myth. For it must be decided
whether the "Lamia" of Poliziano should be assessed as a "literary" or
as a "philosophical" text. This is a question which concerns us when we
consider the metaphoric texts of Humanists.

At first glance one must assert that there is no essential difference between "fable," i.e., "literary narrative," and "philosophical metaphor": in
both cases we are faced with transferences. In "literary fables" flowers
and trees talk, and non-existent "fabulous" creatures, which look like animals
or humans, appear: hypogryphs, mountain spirits, fairies. Poliziano, too,
tells of witches, and lets birds talk.

When analyzing the structure of metaphors, Aristotle maintains that the
"transference" *must not be arbitrary.* It presupposes the "discovery" of a
κοινωνία between both sides of the transference. The real metaphoric "transfer" "*implies insight into the commonness*" [τὸ ὅμοιον θεωρεῖν].[38] "The
transfer has to begin with what they have in common"[39]: only the discovered "commonness" provides the objectivity of the transfer. Aristotle maintains that the metaphoric transfer is not a result of a rational process, but
arises from an ingenious insight into "relationships" by which something
new is put "in front of our eyes" which has not been seen before.[40]

Aristotle gives two examples: he mentions a passage in the *Iliad* where
the poet maintains that the spears of Danai stare out of the ground in order

to revel greedily in human flesh.[41] It is plain that the spears of the Danai have no "greed": they are merely weapons in human hands. But the "transfer" lets us see the cruelty of the deadly tool which rational discourse could disclose only laboriously, and never so perceptively and with such pathos. Only in the area of a battle situation can the special meaning be transferred to the spear.

In his *Rhetoric*[42] Aristotle gives a further example, which he takes from a speech of Pericles and which refers to the dying of Athenian youth in war: youth has vanished from the city as if spring had been expelled from it. This metaphor, which is created in analogy [κατ' ἀναλογίαν],[43] immediately places a very concrete situation in front of our eyes. Its character as "image" affects the passions and surmounts the separation of theory and praxis. Aristotle's thesis culminates in the assertion that philosophy, metaphorical thinking and speaking all have something in common: "It is part of philosophy, too, that he who understands precisely also has insight into the commonness and similarity [τὸ ὅμοιον θεωρεῖν] between the most distinct and distant matters."[44]

If one recognizes—as in the case of Bruni—that the "being-there" must realize itself within the framework of the diverse situations which enunciate the most diverse demands, then it is apparent that the "being-there" (*Daseiende*)—a present participle of the verb "to be" used as a noun—can respond to the various demands only through metaphoric expression, in order to discover itself in its own historicity. The metaphor which has the meaning of a semantic expression with regard to the demand of the experience of the "here" and "now" is a "philosophical metaphor" and not a "literary fable"; correspondingly, the "philomythos" is a philosopher, albeit *not* in the traditional, rationalistic meaning of the term.

In other words, if we recognize that the responses to the demands with which "being-there" realizes itself cannot be achieved through the rational and abstract definition of words, then we are also forced to recognize the primary importance of metaphorical thinking and speaking. But whenever the transfer happens not in order to disclose the demand in its historicity, but only as play, as diversion in the face of the demands which crowd in upon us, then we have either a playful "literary metaphor," or the arbitrary and conventional transfers which deal with practical matters.

We should not forget that according to Aristotle the metaphor unveils something particular (οἰκεῖον)[45] which had been hidden before. The metaphor originates from the desire to "see," to "discover" what is concealed.[46] As essential qualities of the metaphor Aristotle names clarity (τὸ σαφές) because that which is proved by it must be indubitable – and the conjuring up of a feeling of "alienation" (τὸ ξενικόν) insofar as something unexpected and extraordinary is disclosed. He does not give a universal definition of being in its abstractness, but endeavors to disclose being within the framework of historic urging, and in this way demonstrates the identity of philosophical and metaphorical speaking and thinking.

In the fable with which he begins his inaugural lecture, Poliziano maintains (referring to Plutarch) that witches have no eyes.[47] They can, however, put eyes in or take them out like spectacles, and once they have been used they can be kept in a box.[48] Outside their homes, the witches put their eyes in and investigate everything critically.[49] Nothing escapes them. But when they return home, they take their eyes out again, remain blind, and gabble stupidly. Poliziano does not simply place a "literary fable" before us, but casts light on a concrete situation in Florence. His contemporaries, the critics, understand neither his task nor what this new form of philosophizing means. It is the witches who reign in Florence: "Vidistisne . . . unquam Lamias istas, viri florentini?" They put on masks [personatae incedunt],[50] and call Poliziano to account: they maintain that he calls himself a philosopher in an arbitrary manner. But he denies this on principle: "philosophum esse, quod ego profecto non sum."[51]

Similarly, the concluding narrative proves to be not an arbitrary literary fable, but a true philosophical metaphor. The owl as symbol of wisdom reigns no longer: its sharp, evil eye, its cutting beak and its feathers are all that have remained: ". . . noctuarum quidem plumas habent et oculos et rostrum, sapientiam vero non habent."[52] The birds no longer listen to the "real" owl; they become caught on the lime of the mistletoe and so lose their freedom. Within the framework of these metaphors with which he opens and concludes his work, Poliziano deals with the essential themes of his inaugural lecture: what a philosopher, according to the traditional understanding, is, and why, because of that understanding, he does not take himself to be a philosopher: "Videamus ergo primum . . . quod homines philosophum vocant: tum spero facile intelligetis, *non esse me philosophum.*"[53]

The question of what, according to tradition, a philosopher is, he answers ironically. He tells a story about a philosopher from Samos who is said, first of all, to have cut off the tongues of his disciples, whose doctrine is said to be ridiculous; and so on.[54] Only then does Poliziano

identify what one understands traditionally as "philosophy," clearly referring to the model outlined by Plato: a refusal of the relative, the historical,
the sensual in order to maintain the universal and eternal. With reference
to the Pythagorean Architas, Poliziano remarks pointedly that, according
to that understanding of philosophy, "ratio" was attributed to humans as
the highest court of appeals in their task of distinguishing between the signifying words: ". . . mens, quasi regina, quodcumque opus est ratione ex-
cogitationeque perficit . . . significationesque nominum forent et
verborum."[55] Such a rational philosophy asserts that the corporeal is evil.
Therefore, the thesis that the soul lives in the body as in a prison is
justified.[56] Poliziano concludes this outline of traditional philosophy by al-
luding to Plato's parable of the cave.[57]

In view of such a Platonizing understanding of philosophy, Poliziano
explicitly denies that he is a philosopher and confesses to being an "interpres": ". . . certe interpretem profiteor, philosophum non profiteor."[58] According to him, to be an "interpreter" means to be a "grammarian," i.e.,
to be able to identify the meaning of words within the frame-work of varying contexts and therefore in their historicity: "Grammaticorum enim sunt
haec partes, ut *omne scriptorum genus*, poetas, historicos, oratores,
philosophos, medicos, iureconsultos excutiant atque enarrent."[59] He
specifically stresses the misinterpretations and restrictions imposed on the
concept of the grammarian during his own time[60] by identifying the grammarian only with the "litterae"—that is, someone who is an authority in
the field of the trivium. For Poliziano, to be a grammarian means to be
an interpreter—not someone who deduces the definitions of words rationally in accordance with the traditional model of philosophical thinking.
Again, we witness the preeminence of the problem of the word.

3

The New Concept of "Scientia":
Coluccio Salutati (1331–1406)

The turning point in the development from traditional metaphysics to
the specific philosophizing of Humanism occurs with the advent of the
problem of the word (*verba*) in lieu of the question of being (*res*) and its

rational determination. Traditional metaphysics starts from the presupposition of being as something existing per se, and it tries to "fix" and "mark out" rationally the identity of being. If language deviates from this task, it becomes either the expression of the subjective fantasy of a poet, or of rhetorical speaking, which is dependent on time and place. In both cases, language cannot fulfill its philosophical task. Any philosophy which uses rational language plainly represents the endeavor of gaining liberation from the subjective in order to attain the objective and universal. In view of the Humanist's philological task and of the experience of the ambiguity of every word in varying contexts, the significance of words is no longer a rational definition of being, but a response to historical claims in view of which being—subject and object—is discovered in its meaning.

We can now say that while the determination of a word tries to achieve an a-historical realization of language, the philosophical thinking of Humanism endeavors to discover the historicity of the word. Whereas traditional philosophy is metaphysical, Humanistic philosophy is "philologic," and rightfully claims, according to Poliziano, to begin from the love for the word. But towards what new kind of wisdom or "scientia" does Humanism strive? In other words, what new understanding of knowledge and of language may be achieved in the Humanistic tradition if this understanding must be achieved within and through the demands which the "being-there" faces, historically, time and again?[2]

Albertino Mussato identifies wisdom with poetry, without, however, justifying this fundamental thesis. Through his affirmation of the vernacular and through his determination of the original task of poetic language, Dante had—as poet and as orator—emphasized the importance of historical language in lieu of rational and abstract metaphysical language. But he, too, did not give any speculative foundation to his thesis. Petrarch and Boccaccio had tried to affirm the preeminence of poetic wisdom, but had become bogged down in the difficulties arising from traditional thought. We must, therefore, discover whether, and by whom, this principal question of Humanism has been discussed. Only by answering this question can we identify unambiguously the importance of Humanistic philosophy, which was, for a long time, hidden by rationalism.

In his *De laboribus Herculis*[61] Coluccio Salutati not only takes a fresh approach to the defense of the poetic, but also toward a new definition of knowledge, of "scientia." His tract is principally directed against "those in our time who give themselves airs as philosophers,"[62] for it is these, he writes, who "partly have a low esteem of our poetry or deprecate it."[63] Salutati identifies these philosophers with those who imitate the "British" rationalists: "They occupy themselves with the writings of some Britons who are so remote from us, as if our own regions do not offer us enough for our education."[64]

At first glance it is surprising that Salutati occupies himself with a defense of poetry in a book titled *De laboribus Herculis* (The Labors of Hercules), particularly since the defense involves an outline of a new concept of "scientia." But in order to become fully conscious of the importance of his project we should not forget that in classical tradition Hercules is the symbol of human existence, because as the conqueror of the hostile forces of nature he discloses the human world. In contrast to its traditional rationalistic structure Salutati identifies the concept of "scientia" with the Muses. He stresses emphatically that no one particular muse, but only all nine together are able to lead us in the search[65] for and help us to achieve a "doctrine perfectionem."[66]

The first three muses whom Salutati introduces concern the *preconditions* for a realization of "scientia." The first condition to achieve knowledge is the desire for fame, which is in the hands of the Muse Clio: "Prima namque cogitationi discere cupientium primum occurrit *fame celebritas que gloria est*."[67] The second condition is the enjoyment of one's own labors; this aspect is dominated by the Muse Euterpe: "Euterpen, quod Latine dicit nichil aliud esse quam '*bene delectans.*' "[68] Finally, man's striving for knowledge must be characterized by perseverance in his studies; this is the realm of Melpomene: "Melpomenem . . ., 'Meditationem faciens permanere.' "[69]

With this point, Salutati has raised a methodological problem: which road will lead to "scientia?" It is striking that Salutati attaches so much weight to the "attitude" of the student rather than to rules of a rational kind, as happens traditionally. What is important is the recognition that the learner depends on the primary "powers" of the Muses and not on the "ratio." Such demands have all the character of an appeal, and it is in this sense that they are "music."

The second group with which Salutati is concerned does not have to do with the "attitude" which leads to knowledge, but rather with the essence and structure of knowledge. "Scientia" implies foremost the "percipere" which Salutati identifies with the power of Thalia, the fourth Muse, who sows the seeds of knowledge.[70] Our knowledge begins with sense phenomena, which provide the material for the disclosure of our world. The senses are the tools of a disclosing power, but they are in no way specific for the unveiling and for the claims which are specific to human beings. In order to achieve "scientia" it is not sufficient only to "perceive"; it is necessary to "preserve" the perceived: "parum est didicisse nisi commemores iam percepta";[71] Salutati directs our attention to the fifth Muse, Polyhymnia, with respect to "remembering much."[72]

However, the preservation of that which appears is not congruent with "scientia." Salutati stresses that all efforts to achieve "scientia" would be in vain if man were to remain in the realm of phenomena and of remembering them, i.e., within the framework of the claims of the two preceding powers. Tradition makes "ratio" the essential element in the quest for "scientia." By way of contrast, Salutati's thesis is that no one is cognizant [doctus non est] who does not penetrate to *the finding of the similar* [in similium inventionem erumpere].[73]

The appeal of the knowledge to which man is subjected is identified with the demand made by Erato, the sixth Muse, whose Greek name Salutati relates to "finding" (*invenire*),[74] to the "finding of the similar" [similia inveniens].[75] What kind of cognizance does Salutati mean when he ascribes the essential element of cognition to the power of Erato, and not to "ratio?" It is "the finding of similarities" [de similibus in similia se transferre, . . . similia invenire]; that is, "scientia" is not identified with a rational definition of being whose first task is the rational determination of the "res."

For Salutati the μεταφέρειν, the ingenious finding of similarities (*similitudines*), is the starting point of "scientia"; it implies a rich and varied language which is essentially distinct from rational language. And because the discovering of relationships is not a matter for the "ratio" but for the "ingenium," "ingenious" thinking is the essence of "scientia," i.e., of inventive, indicating thinking and not of deduction and proof. Both forms of science have already been distinguished in principle by Cicero in his references to the "ars inveniendi" and the "ars demonstrandi."[76] The latter presupposes the "finding" of the premises which are necessary for the syllogism; the whole syllogistic process is attributed to the "ratio." Cicero maintains explicitly: "We find in this art [*ars demonstrandi*] no direction for the discovery of truth [nullum est praeceptum, quo modo verum inveniatur], but only in what fashion the argument should be carried out" [sed tantum est, quo modo iudicetur].[77] The first art does not show any rational character; it is essentially "ingenious."[78] The ingenium discovers "relationships," "similitudines": "Comparabile autem est, quod in rebus diversis *similem* aliquam rationem continet."[79]

The μεταφέρειν is, therefore, possible only on the basis of the activity of the "ingenium,"[80] which brings about the "finding of the *similitudines*." For Salutati the metaphor is therefore the original form of cognizance. The metaphor provides the transition to knowledge from the information which is provided by the senses (*percipere*) and which is kept present by the memory (*memoria*). It is here that the breakthrough into a new reality occurs: here the metamorphosis of man takes place.

If the metaphor is therefore the essence of poetic speech, we also find in Salutati the first arguments in favor of the thesis which the last Humanistic philosopher, G. B. Vico, will use three hundred years later in his *New Science*. Through the "clearing" (*Lichtung*) of the metaphor the abundance of being is disclosed in its human significance; for this very reason Vico will maintain that metaphoric thinking and speaking were "necessary modes of expression of all the first poetic nations."[81]

Salutati explains that through poetry humans have been diverted "from that which is offered to them by their senses [a sensibus taliter traducebant]" and that because of this they believed in something that was in fact the opposite of that which they had experienced with their own eyes.[82] But it is also this "deception" which lifts human beings out of the condition of "feritas." Must this work of the activity of the "ingenium" not properly be called a "deceit?" Salutati does not answer this question by means of speculative argumentation; instead he points to the consequences of the work of the creative poet: its result is the human community in its historicity.[83]

In this openness and unconcealedness which the poetic predication establishes, gods, things, all living beings make their appearance in their original significance: "From the height of their ingenium the seers [the poets] observe three things through which they illuminate their poems as with lights [quibus sua poemata quasi luminibus exornaverunt], God, the world, and everything animate [deum, mundum et animantia], in order to give a name to everything which is called a living being."[84] It is an invisible god who reveals himself differently in varying historical forms in different places and times: "Because [the poets] observe that God, the builder of the world, has accomplished everything in his wisdom . . . and that *wisdom is nothing but the godhead itself,* they called the god by different names although they felt that he was one and the same. No one should therefore be in any doubt that in spite of the great number of gods the poets never thought of many gods, they gave the one god different names because of differences in his tasks, times and places."[85]

Rooted in this tradition, Vico will declare at the end of the Humanist tradition that the earliest human beings, incapable of rational thinking (i.e., of the formation of generic notions), "felt the necessity to create poetic characters" (generic notions or universals created by fantasy) in order to relate the species back to certain models or ideal portraits, that is, each species to its resemblant genre.[86] The first tales and myths gain their disclosing function because only in them do the differing sensual phenomena, actions, and things become apparent in their human significance.

The poetic word is an expression of the original and specific human endeavor to attribute significance to the frightening might of Being, which always reveals itself in different forms of human historicity. Only in the attempt to overcome this might is the human historic world able to emerge. For this reason, Vico has pointed out that in their investigations of the philosophy of antiquity, the philosophers and philologists should have started from poetic wisdom, the first truth of heathendom, "not from an abstract and rational wisdom of the learned scholars."[87]

Finally, we should look at the last three Muses or powers in whose sphere, according to Salutati's thesis, the human world discloses itself. The seventh Muse, Terpsichore, represents the function of "ratio"; that which has been opened by Erato (the sixth Muse) through metaphor must now be fixed in its consequences [super omnia discretionis oportet habere judicium]. Only in the light of the disclosing function of the eighth Muse, Urania (the Heavenly, *caelestis*) can that which has been disclosed by metaphor and fixed as consequence by "ratio" be defined in the framework of a single horizon: one encompassing world. Only then, under the guidance of the ninth Muse, Calliope, can the temporal world, with its gods, its institutions, and its history, become the subject of a poem, the "optime melos."

4

The "Astounding" Word:
Giovanni Pontano (1426–1503)

Our thesis states that the originality of the specific philosophical significance of Humanism lies neither in the revival of traditional neo-Platonic metaphysics, nor in a new anthropology which puts all emphasis on man and his immanent value. Instead, it lies in a philosophy which arises from and consists of the problematic of the word. It is Giovanni Pontano who not only stresses the originality of the problem of the word, but also the function of the poetic word in its fullest import.

His fundamental thesis is a discussion, within the framework of a theological problematic, of the original creation of being and of the essence of the divine: ". . . sic mecum ipse et rerum creationem perscrutor . . . et Deum ipsum contemplor."[88] He maintains explicitly that being discloses itself in and through the word: "quae sunt cuncta quidem verbo creasse."[89] Chariteus, an orator in Pontano's dialogue *Aegidius*, poses the question of the essence of the word as an introduction to a thesis on the preeminence of the poetic word. Discussing Hermes Trismegistus, Chariteus affirms solemnly that he had left Platonic thinking behind.[90] Pontano not only gives prominence to the creative character of the divine word [creationem ipsam provenisse crediderim ex verbo Dei],[91] but he also explicitly identifies the word with the Divine: "nihil existeret omnino aliud praeterquam *verbum, quod ipsum Deus quidem erat.*"[92] Human fate rests in the power of the word: "Itaque ut *fatum* a fando, idest a dicendo deductum est."[93]

Pontano points out that, in general, theorists discuss the problem of the divine creation of beings with reference to Aristotle [. . . cum audeat Aristoteles profiteri],[94] usually stressing the "deficiency" in matter, which some authors, the so-called "Aristotelians," term "privation." Pontano maintains that a theory of the creation of beings explained with reference to Aristotle's doctrine of the four causes is a speculative attempt by people of little religiosity: "Haec parum pii homines ita se habere"; in the divine word, matter and form are inseparable: "in divino illo edicto 'Fiat' et materiam inesse et formam."[95]

Therefore, Pontano goes back to Cicero, who, regarding the notion of "carere" (traditionally used to define matter), asserts the following: some-

thing cannot "want" (*carere*) if it is not already something distinct: "Tullius
. . . ait non posse eum qui ipse not sit re ulla carere."[96] From this Pontano concludes "that in my opinion the expression 'carentia,' rather than
'privatio,' defines matter exactly, because matter *needs* form, and so forces
itself out of its own nature in order to achieve form" [Propriam itaque ap-
pellationem esse arbitror *carentiam* cum materia indigeat forma quam suapte
natura cupiat sibi inesse].[97] Pontano's thesis of the divinity and originality of the word thus clearly derives from his insistence on the inseparability of the "res" and the "verba," of "matter" and "form" within the Divine:
the disclosing of being is understood as the appeal of the Divine in the word.

However, in the Humanist tradition which we have followed to this point,
the original word is the poetic word. But in what kind of word does Being
originally speak? In Pontano's basic thesis, the poetic language, not the
rational, is original. The poetic word appears in the realm of the "admira-
bile" and "astounding." The deeper structure of the poetic expression and
its original disclosing function consists in the inner connection between
the "mirabile" object of poetry and the word which conjures up "admiration." The poet ". . . in ammirabili re ennarranda tractum se ammiratione
ipsa ab initio statim ostendit."[98] In a different dialogue we read: ". . . poetae sive finem sive officium esse bene atque excellenter loqui ad admirationem."[99]

But what is the object of the "mirabile," of the "admirable," the "astounding?" Is it the transcendent which — as in the Platonic and neo-Platonic
understanding — exists in an eternal world? The original task of poetry and
its speculative importance for Pontano becomes understandable only if
we exactly determine the essence, the philosophical function and the sphere
of the "mirabile," under whose "pointing" sign the poetic word arises. Therefore we have to put the question in the following way: does the "mirabile"
belong to a purely theoretical, contemplative and "extra-historical" sphere,
in accordance with the model of Platonic thinking? Would, therefore, in
this case, the traditional interpretation of Humanism as Platonism be
justified?

In answering this question we should refer to Pontano's exegesis of a
passage from a work of poetry. When interpreting the passage from the
Aeneid[100] in which Vergil describes the eruption of the Aetna, Pontano
stresses that Vergil's poetic word does not intend to portray the "reality"
of the volcano so much as to present exactly how Aeneas experiences the
concrete situation, which he brings to life principally through the senses.

Pontano states: "Vergil himself stresses that the Aetna did not serve him as a model" [Aetnae montis naturam id consilii non fuisse sibi Virgilius ipse prae se fert].[101] In the following sentences he formulates this thought more precisely: in his poetic word Vergil does not start with the Aetna as his "material" which he then sets out to describe [ut vellet pro assumpta at quodammodo destinata materia describere].[102] In his description Vergil is not interested in representing something "similar": "at noster nulla huiusmodi similitudine usus";[103] nevertheless, the poem "sticks closely to the subject matter" [rebus ipsis inhaerens].[104] In a different place we read: "a rei natura non recedit."[105]

The hermeneutics of poetic reality have their roots in the sphere of the problematic of the word, which is the expression of an unsettling experienced "here" and "now": "ut horroris plenam verbis suis ante oculos ponere animisque . . . ipsam inquam rem suis atque heroicis verbis enarrat."[106] In his interpretation of the Vergilian passage, Pontano puts the accent first on hearing, on sound—the loudness of the "booming Aetna" as experienced by Aeneas when he enters the Sicilian harbor,[107] and then on that which is disclosed to the view; through this gradual building up of sense experiences the miracle impresses itself very strongly on us: "magis ac magis rei miraculo afficeret."[108] Poetry has the function of making manifest the miracle, the admirable, the unfoundable, and, therefore, un-fathomable in the "here" and "now," not in the contemplation of the abstract.

In all this we should not forget the original meaning of the Greek term θαῦμα and of the related verb θαυμάζειν, both expressions for the "mirabile," for the "miraculous," for that which fills us with admiration, and as such conjures up "wonderment" and, at the same time, the urge to know. Both the Greek noun as well as the verb point to the "astonishment" and the "veneration" of that which seems inexplicable to us and imposes a demand on us. In his *Metaphysics* Aristotle emphasizes the relationship between astonishment and the origin of philosophy: "For it is astonishment which initially and even today leads people to philosophize . . . whoever is unable to explain something and starts wondering [ἀπορῶν καὶ θαυμάζων], believes that he does not understand; in this regard the friend of myths is also a philosopher, for myth consists of miraculous happenings."[109]

Essential elements which help determine our problematic come together in the genealogy of "Thauma" and "Iris" in Greek mythology: "Thauma" is the son of Gaia, the creatrix of all earthly things, and so he stands in an immediate relationship to the birth, flowering, and passing of everything in existence. Iris, the daughter of "Thauma," is the personification of the rainbow, the multicolored bridge spanning celestial and terrestrial beings. In the wonderment about the rainbow which unites heaven and earth—that is, through the very linguistic expression, through the word (Iris—ἐρειν)—Greek mythological thinking has expressed the function of the "miraculous" in a metaphor: the "wondrous" word has become the root of the disclosing metamorphosis of the human world. The philosophical metaphor is not "literary play," but a philosophical narrative; the myth is no fable: the disclosure of the "res" into its significance takes place in the "pointing" and "pronouncing" word, not in the demonstrating word.

Pontano's thesis that the "miraculous" is the subject of poetry—and that the poetic word conjures up "wonderment" in order to disclose being in its original significance—is not "literary." In his dialogues *Aegidius* and *Actius* Pontano maintains that it is through the poetic word that man steps out of the "dark forest" in order to found human society. Furthermore, he asserts that the source of any language is the poetic expression: in it rests the essence and the original function of the words: "Quo fit ut omne dicendi genus a poetica manaverit. Nam et primi doctorum omnium cum extiterint poetae, omnia quoque carmine ac numeris sunt complexi testisque horum omnium est Homerus, qui quantum ubique dicendo valeat et suspiciunt docti et admirantur indocti."[110]

The Muses, the goddesses of poetry, disclose being, for no other divine power can claim "scire quae sit rerum quae in terra fiunt, geruntur gignunturque natura."[111] Poetry was first to choose the divine for its theme and to sing its praise [. . . princeps de Deo et disseruit et eius laudes cecinit] and to introduce holy rituals; for this reason the first poets have been called priests.[112] Pontano salutes poetry in the following solemn words: "Salve igtur, doctrinarum omnium mater foecundissima"[113]; for it was poetry that first taught us to care for all things human [docuitque habere rerum humanarum curam], to treat the righteous benevolently, and to punish the unjust.[114] Poetry is theology. Through poetry that power is disclosed which opens up a space for human action and creates a "clearing" (*Lichtung*) in the primeval forest, and that clearing will be the stage for history.[115]

It is poetry which overcomes transience in time, for man finds himself in his deepest essence again and again in and through the solemn words of poetry: "Tu enim mortalitati occurristi inventorum ac scriptorum tuorum perpetuitate."[116] Poetry is rooted in a wonderment and admiration which has neither "hyperuranic" nor "suprahistorical'" nor "theoretical" character: it has as its object the un-fathomable which makes itself known in history.

Pontano is, therefore, in constant dispute with those who are unable to draw from the sphere of the "mirabile" the significance of the poetic word, and who merely try to deduce the meaning of the words with the help of the rational process. "Friend Favorinus, go back to your philosophy in which you can talk about the syllogism [ad philosophiam tuam redi, de syllogismo] . . . for you know neither the figures of speech nor the expressions of the poets."[117] Pontano's following criticism is also clear: "If you had read Cicero, not only would you have learnt Latin but you would also have been able to make an exact judgment about the ingenium of the writers and their work."[118]

5
The Unity of Poetry, Rhetoric, and History

As the motto for Pontano's discussion of essence and the function of poetry, we could take the following sentence from St. Augustine: "Plane incredibilius, quia mirabilius; et mirabilius, quia potentius."[119] In Pontano's discussion the question of poetry is given a significance which transcends by far any mere "literary theory." His conception of the problem, which begins with the thesis of the preeminence of the poetic word, is far removed in essence from any traditional metaphysico-rational thinking. Pontano is conscious of this fact, and in his dialogue *Aegidius* one of the interlocutors expresses the hope that before his death he might see the establishment and flourishing of a "Latin philosophy," which arises from the problem of and the caring for the word, and which puts an end to the polemics of the rationalistic discussions, in order to make serene and detached philosophical dialogues possible.[120] This desired "Latin philosophy" is explicitly identified with a thinking which does not start from abstract rational universal principles, but from "a concrete contemplation of things, times, personalities and places."[121]

The original disclosure of the significance of being—which takes place not through logical processes but in and through the poetic word—forces the Humanist to clarify the relationship between rhetoric and poetry. In his *Actius* Pontano states that "rhetoric has taken the sublime and dignified rhythm of its language from the poets who in fact have been the first teachers of oratory."[122]

The experience of the unfathomable, which is revealed in admiration and astonishment, is expressed in the eulogy. Referring to Cicero, Pontano maintains that poetry and rhetoric—of which the eulogy is but one form—belong together: "oratori poetam . . . utriusque communes sunt laudationes."[123] The "eulogia" belongs to poetry even when it deals with the particular, for it is precisely through the particular that the "eminent" is revealed.[124]

But if, on the one hand, the miraculous is expressed in the form of eulogy, and if, on the other hand, the eulogy (together with forensic and political speech) belongs to the realm of rhetoric, what then is the distinction between rhetoric and poetry? In forensic as well as political matters, the orator gains victory in the context of the concrete situation—that is, in view of the judgment of the judge and of the political decision of the community—while through his eulogy the orator can become famous beyond the limits of the present moment: "Oratoris scilicet ut persuadeat iudici, poetae ut admirationem sibi ex audiente ac legente comparet, cum ille pro victoria nitatur, hic pro fama et gloria."[125] When one fails to remember the original function of poetry and its close connection with rhetoric, an ominous separation between rhetoric and knowledge occurs: "dicendi laus a disciplinarum cognitione seiuncta fuerit."[126] Pontano deplores the fact that his contemporaries either follow rhetoric without recognizing its philosophical significance or, conversely, fail to recognize the rhetorical structure of philosophy: "eloquentiae studiosos aut nullam aut perexiguam impendisse philosophiae operam, ipsos vero philosophos eloquentiae penitus esse ignaros atque utinam non et hostes."[127] Pontano expresses the wish that philosophy might achieve a harmonious relationship with science and theology: ". . . eloquentia cum doctrina tum naturali tum divina in gratiam redeat."[128]

If, however, poetry does not seek the unfathomable and astonishing in a suprahistorical reality, but in that reality which is disclosed through the becoming of man and the claims which history makes upon him, does there then also exist any relationship between poetry and historiography? Pontano answers this question with the thesis that history is poetry in prose: ". . . historiam poeticam pene solutam esse. . . ."[129] In order to understand this theory we must return to his earlier one, namely, to the theory that historiography consists of two elements: of the "res," the report of what has happened, and of the "verba," the language appropriate to it.[130] We therefore have to deal first with the matter (*res*) of history and after that with the language historiography uses.

In this context Pontano maintains that every "res" — in its happening — has its own order and disposition (*ordo et dispositio*), because some events precede and others follow and exist in a casual connection: from this we conclude that the historical narrative should represent the causal order: ". . . de rebus quidem ipsis existit enarratio; verbis autem series earum contexitur."[131] Tradition shows that the fame of the historiographer and the praise he earns spring from the ability to present all events as parts of a single organism in a successive sequence.[132]

It is clear that the causes and the arising consequences are fundamental to the historical situation. In any case, one should not overlook the fact that the goal of the actor results from the evaluation of the historical situation in which he finds himself: the evaluation cannot be derived casually from the situation. For example, the siege of a city is the result or the consequence of a chain of causes and effects in a time sequence. This is the reason why Pontano insists that the historian must discover not only the immediate, but also the older and hidden causes of given situation.[133] However, this is still not sufficient. The historian also has to discover the debated decisions, the *evaluation* of situation. Only then does a decision become understandable: ". . . lectores ipsi apertius doceantur de altercationum causis consiliorumque ac sententiarum diversitate."[134] Therefore, the historian not only has to describe the causal connection of events but also the actors' interpretation of the given situation. For this reason Pontano indicates that the historian has to discover the moral attitudes, the characters and traditions of the strategist, the politician and statesman. He points out that Livy directs all his attention to the traditions surrounding the character of Hannibal. Similarly, Sallustius does the same with regard to Jugurtha.[135] Therefore, the "res" of the historian contains two aspects: one is the *elucidation of the historical situation* in its causal concatenation; the other is the "ingenium," the *adjudication* of which differs in every individual case and is expressed with respect to the chosen goal of the action. The sole presentation of the causal connection of events does not explain the "res" of history.

But what does Pontano mean when he defines historiography as poetry in prose? This thesis does not arise out of "literary" or "formal" theories. The poetic word represents the original language. The "miraculous" does not announce itself as a sign of "suprahistorical" reality but as a sign of the original object of astonishment which man experiences "here" and "now" in a different situation. As this situation is at the same time the object of historiography, it becomes clear that poetry and historiography are conditionally and essentially connected. This leads Pontano to maintain that our ancestors already took historiography to be "quasi solutam poeticam putavere."[136]

The words of the language chosen and applied by the historian have to respond to the concrete situation and its evaluation. For this very reason the logical truths which are valid in all places and at all times are not the object of the historians. Pontano maintains that the historian's word, his adjectives, verbs, and the rhythm of the sentences have to be adjusted time and again to the concrete situation: ". . . videndum est . . . ut ea sint propria, accomodata, delecta, usitata bonis ab auctoribus, *pro loco ac re sumpta,* quanquam interdum, pro rei magnitudine, a poetis quoque mutuanda ea sunt. . . ."[137]

Precisely because the language of the historian should not be rational, it makes use of "ornamenta," the expressive "embellishments" which respond to the varying circumstances; "ornamenta" which *per se* have no justification in the area of logical thinking and speaking: "Ad haec summa ea cura expolienda exornandaque, ut nec forma ornatu careat extrinseco nec ornatus appareat aut negligenter adhibitus aut alienus a forma."[138]

The "ornatus" is not an external "decoration" but an essential means for making "apparent" the particularity of the *temporal and local* given. This can never be gained by a purely casual concatenation of a sequence of events, as in a chronicle. This is exactly what Pontano refers to when, following Cicero, he distinguishes between the annals of the Pontifices and their history proper: ". . . meminisse potes Ciceronem exigere maius quiddam in historia quam quod in annalibus pontificum . . . ."[139] In the following passage he gives an example of the language of the historian: "How should Hannibal, may I ask, have traversed the river Rhone without the clamor, without the shouting, the mutiny of sailors, without the anxiety and the terror of the elephants, and without the plunging of the animals into the whirlpool of the river? Could it have been crossed without thunder and lightening, clouds and frost, and was it not necessary that he should have destroyed everything in his way?"[140]

Potano stresses that the "objectivity" of the historian, the "truth" which serves him as goal, can be reached only through the elucidation of the "situation" and by taking into account its "ingenious" evaluation by the strategist or the politician. Only in this manner is it possible to gain distance from the subjectivity of the narration and to achieve the "gravitas" of historical reports: ". . . gravitas item ea quae addat explicationi ac dictis pondus quaeque et auctorem rerum et scriptorem commendet."[141] Only through this insight (of the need to change the words according to the varying historical events) can the correct "collocatio" be achieved.[142] Poetry and historiography enthuse the reader through an "embellishment" (*ornatu*) of the facts[143] in order to reveal the concrete situation [ante oculos ponat],[144] and thus let it shine eternally: ". . . quod susceperit dicendum illustrare et quoad possit sempiternum id efficere."[145]

CHAPTER THREE

The Primacy of the "Litterae"
Guarino Veronese (1374–1460)

1
The Medieval Tradition: Music and Poetry
as "Integumentum" of the True and Eternal

WE HAVE DRAWN ATTENTION TO THE FOUR QUALITIES WHICH DANTE ascribes to poetic, metaphoric language: it is "illuminating"; it is "grounding"; it is in need of space for its activity; and it creates that space where the rules of a language are determined on poetry's own basis. We can, therefore, speak of poetry as the foundation of language. With this thesis, the specific philosophical problematic of Humanism begins.

Mussato maintains that poetry is the first theology, indeed an "altera philosophia." Salutati puts forward the thesis in his *De laboribus Herculis* that "scientia" is not rooted in rational activity, but originates in the realm of metaphoric language: the discovery, the "inventio" of "similitudines" discloses the meaning of beings. The "tropological" experience of philology prevents Bruni from acknowledging the priority of the rational definition of an expression; Poliziano refuses to be called a philosopher in the traditional meaning of the word. He demands for himself the title of "expounder," of "interpres." Pontano points toward the "admirable" character of the poetic word: without starting from an ontological, metaphoric foundation, he, too, attributes to poetry the task of opening the realm of history.

Medieval philosophy proceeds from an opposing starting point: its problem is that of a rational definition of being that goes back to causes, to "ideas" which disclose the essence (οὐσία) of being. This is a rational, abstract definition because it disregards any relation to time and space in order to achieve a truth valid everywhere and always. Here we find the priority of the "res" over the "verbum," for the word acquires its meaning only on the basis of its rational definition.

In accordance with this understanding, medieval thinking is above all intent on tracing back any art form to the realm of the non-historic, the eternal. One of the arts, music, gains its legitimation only insofar as it mirrors the harmony of beings and therefore the eternal and universal. With respect to music, the Middle Ages go back to Pythagorean theory: different sounds result in accordance with the length of a vibrating cord. This length can be measured mathematically, and music is thus anchored in numerically ordered universal relations. These relations express the eternal order of the "cosmos," the harmony of the celestial bodies. Because of its mathematical foundation, music is assigned to the realm of disciplines dealing with numbers and measurements, that is, the *Quadrivium*, which contains geometry, mathematics, astrology and music.

Isidore of Seville (died 636) maintains that nothing can exist without musical order and that without music no science can be perfect. The world is ordered by mathematical proportions; the movements of the heavens are harmonious. Since music exercises and influences the passions, it is therefore the task of music to return the passions to the realm of order, of measured proportions: "sine musica nulla disciplina potest esse perfecta ... Musica movet affectus, provocat in diversum habitum sensus."[1] Isidore derives the term "ars" from "artus" because art is based on fixed rules.[2]

If music, for instance, song, expresses something relative, subjective, something that is bound to time and space and is, therefore, something historic, it is entitled to do so only if it tries to express human despair over the unattainability of the eternal. To prove this point we could use a "planctus" from the thirteenth century on the fate of Samson, or the death-dances from the fourteenth century which had been occasioned by the virulent plague in Europe in 1347, or a "Miserere" from the Elizabethan age.

Adelard of Bath (first half of the twelfth century) reminds us that it was Pythagoras who first distinguished between the music of the world, of man and of instruments. He expressly maintained that music does not originate from the senses, but from reason [easque ipsas non sensuali judicio, quo nulla subtilitas cernitur, sed rationali arbitrio dividit].[3]

Medieval philosophers, quite conscious of the fact that the roots of poetry do not lie in the rational but in the fantastic, the imaginative and the metaphoric, worried about the function of poetry. Isidore of Seville talks about poetry negatively: "The poets called their fables after 'to fabulate' because they are not facts, but only mirages produced by words" [Fabulas poetae a *fando* nominaverunt, quia non sunt res factae, sed tantum loquendo fictae].[4] poetry does not spring from "ratio." Aristotle derives fantasy from φῶς – light [ὄνομα ἀπὸ τοῦ φάους] – because we cannot see without light.[5] Fantasy is legitimized only by the fact that it brings to the soul the material for the rational process. Fantasy is therefore under the dominance of "ratio," otherwise fantasy would give us only "fables" without any claim to truth.

Richard of St. Victor (died 1173) expresses the same thought in the following manner: "Reason could never rise to the contemplation of the invisible if fantasy did not represent and indicate the forms of visible things" [Nunquam enim ratio ad invisibilium contemplationem assurgeret, nisi ei imaginatio rerum visibilium formas repraesentando exhiberet].[6] Similarly, Boethius stresses the primacy of the *ratio,* which brings to unity the manifold material given by the senses: "sensus invenit quidem confusa . . . accipit vero ratione integritatem."[7] Bonaventure states explicitly that language has to be dominated by the "res" which is determined rationally, and not the "res" determined by language: "non sermoni res, sed rei sermo est subjectus."[8]

All the difficulties of the humanists – which we have already mentioned when discussing Petrarch and Boccaccio – arise, when, attempting to legitimize metaphoric thinking and speaking, they confront this position. Poetry is justified only if it expresses "truth," albeit not in rational but in metaphoric language: the metaphor is permissible as an "alternative form" to express that which is true. Hrabanus Maurus (780–856) writes: "The poet's task is to transpose real events into a different form through an indirect presentation, and with decorum" [Officium poetae in eo est, ut ea, quae vere gesta sunt, in alias species obliquis figurationibus cum decore aliqo conversa transducat].[9]

The "alternative form" mentioned above is only the "external integument." The truth lies hidden behind it. In his famous commentary on Vergil's *Aeneid,* which gained such great importance during the Middle Ages, Bernardus Silvestris (twelfth century) maintains: "The integument is a form of description in which the insight into truth is cloaked into a fairy-tale-like narrative which, therefore, is also called a veil" [integumentum est genus demonstrationis sub fabulosa narratione veritatis involvens intellectum, unde et iam dicitur involucrum].[10]

2
The New Concept of Knowledge and of Teaching:
The Task of the "Litterae"

Traditional philosophy places its principal emphasis on the rational determination of being, that is, on a definition which abstracts from all time and space relations, and, therefore, from all historical ties. The rational process thus leads to a knowledge which culminates in a theory of universals: the meaning of being results exclusively from universal categories which the philosopher starts from in order to define being *a priori* (that is, as non-historical). From this results the debate between the nominalists and realists, and the discussion of whether the categories are to be taken as something real, something existing in themselves—insofar as they disclose being—or only as pure names. For this kind of philosophy the problem of poetry and of rhetoric is hardly of any speculative importance.

Johannes Scotus Eriugena (810–877) had already written that rhetoric and grammar "do not treat the rules of language according to the things [the *res*], but according to human habits or special human conditions which are far removed from reality" [non de rerum natura tractare videntur, sed vel de regulis humanae vocis, quam non secundum naturam, sed secundum consuetudinem loquentium].[11] Through this tight interconnection between grammar and logic there arose conflicts which—as Valla later criticizes—will lead to a haggling about words, "verborum controversia."

Two consequences result from such an understanding: the teaching of the different disciplines must be principally located in an ontology; and no philosophical function can be attributed to the "litterae," such as poetry. Sciences like history can fulfill their function only inasmuch as they present positive or negative examples for insights which have already been reached through rational thinking. Because Humanism no longer starts from a rational definition of being, it carries out a complete reversal of philosophy which is far more radical than the so-called "Copernican revolution" of the Cartesian or idealistic thinking of modern times.

The problem of Humanism is that of the original appeal which continuously forces itself upon us in new ways. In varying situations the words responds to this appeal. And as this problem arises, fantasy gains renewed importance. Traditionally, it is interpreted as the faculty of φαίνεσθαι, of appearing, of the being stepping into light, insofar as it forms an εἰκασία, an image which resembles the real. In its turn, the image provides the rational process with the memory, the material from which it derives the universal, the concept.

But εἰκασία may also be understood as that which appears through an analogy between the sense appearance and the original appeal; or analogy which is discovered by the activity of the ingenium, that is, as "similtudines" which make metaphoric thinking and speaking possible. Thus the problem of the primacy of the "ingenious" (the "inventory" capacity) takes the place of the rational process; and with this problem comes the recognition of the necessity of responding to the demands to which the "being-there" (*Da-sein*) is exposed in the here and now of concrete situations. This recognition results in the importance of history and, therefore, of the necessity to develop a new concept of teaching. This is the problem faced by Guarino Veronese.

Generally speaking, this pedagogue has not been given credit as a systematic thinker: his educational activities at the court of the Duke of Este are praised, and his new methods of textual criticism are emphasized, and it is often stressed that many of his disciples helped to spread the humanist spirit all over Europe; but his theory of knowledge, which differs from the traditional view and which is intimately linked to his conception of teaching, is underrated.

In one of his letters Guarino summarizes the traditional view of knowledge. One acquires knowledge by starting from a proposition (*pro-positio*), the validity of which must be proven [quod intendimus . . . haec ratio dici solet]: only through this process do we gain knowledge [demonstremus verum]. It must be emphasized that—for Guarino—this rational process concerns the truth of "being": "*quid sit* quod probare volumus."[12] Traditional teaching therefore moves in the realm of "demonstration." Educational activity consists of providing reasons for the rational definition of being. If these reasons are unknown to the disciple, he is demonstrably ignorant. Accordingly, the student has to remain completely passive vis-à-vis the teacher. Such a pedagogy is, in its abstract rationality, hardly able to reach the passions of the student or influence his behavior and actions. Thus the inadequacy of rational language becomes apparent: "If I try to demonstrate with reasons that my interlocutor is wrong, my efforts will remain without success" [Quos si aliqua ex parte ratione refellere conabor, inutiles conatus erunt].[13]

Guarino rejects this theory and the corresponding pedagogy. In lieu of a rational theory of being which implies an ontological metaphysics, he puts the study of the "litterae": "I hardly believe that someone is a human being if he does not honor the litterae, does not love them, does not embrace them, does not seize them and completely immerse himself in them" [Hominem medius fidius non esse arbitror qui litteras non diligit non amat non amplectitur, non arripiat, non sese in earum haustu prorsus immergat].[14] The "litterae" represent the highest endeavors of mankind: "Nihil enim et praesentibus annis et futurae aetati melius commodius amoenius praestare potes."[15] They provide the reasons for the conduct of a proper life, "bene vivendi rationes": "Ex litterarum studio optimae *bene vivendi rationes* comparari queunt."[16] Through the "litterae" humans not only become wiser (*doctior*), but also better (*melior*): "When I ask you what you are doing, I would like to receive the following answer from you: I read, I study, I learn, and I am anxious to become wiser and better day by day" [ut in dies doctior ac melior sim].[17]

History, poetry, and rhetoric, which are traditionally excluded from philosophy, are the preconditions for reaching the "ratio vivendi": "historiae cognitionem et reliquas bonas artis quasi necessarium eruditionis et *bene vivendi* cumulum adoptasti."[18] The "litterae" are elevated to the dignity of "ingenious" and "innate" abilities: "Cum igitur ex litterarum studiis et ingenuis artibus decus ornamenta mores, recte vivendi normam comparari cognosceres."[19] Traditional philosophy is not excluded from pedagogy, but it is accompanied by poetry, jurisprudence, the "litterae sacrae," history and rhetoric. For this reason Guarino draws on Homer, Pindar, Sophocles, Vergil, Ovid, and, from among the historians, on Herodotus, Sallust, and Livy. Of the philosophers he mentions Plato, Aristotle and Lucretius, and of medieval authors, St. Augustine, Hieroymus, and Lactantius. Scholastic philosophers, however, are conspicuously absent from his writings.

The "litterae" make humans more knowledgeable, and are the precondition for action: "ipsam disciplinam tibi patriam tibi parentem tibi nutricem tibi nobilitatem adoptasti et sic adoptasti, ut emineas et doctissimus antecellas; nec vero antecellere satis habuisti, nisi praecepta in actum deduxisses."[20] The reading of literary texts provides us with examples and testimonies: "Eius lectio . . . ad pulcherrimam vitae instituta . . . imitatione invitabat et exemplis"; "illis vero *testibus et exemplis* . . . instruatur et corroboretur."[21] But in what sense can Guarino take "examples" to be "testimonies?" The "ratio vivendi" is not to be found in any ontology: above all it is a matter of the interpretation of texts. What does this mean?

3

"Doctrina Exemplorum" and Historical Thinking: "Actio" and "Virtus"

Traditionally, we use an example in order to clarify an already worked out theory; the example does not lead to knowledge, but presupposes it. In contrast, Guarino takes an example to mean a "testimony" in the exact meaning of the word: we learn something not through abstract rational theory, but by being the "witness" to an "event." Examples are not isolated and abstract "images" or "ideas," but insights into the successful or failed response to an appeal which demands to be fulfilled "here" and "now." As such, the example is the "contemplatio" not of an abstract but of a concrete drama whose action takes place in history: "contemplatores suos ad probitatis aemulationem exuta ignavia stimulent."[22] It is a "putting-in-front-of-our-eyes," a recourse to historical "evidence," an "indication."

He who educates himself through examples as testimonies is, at the same time, obliged to respond in his own life to the demands which confront him: "testes quasi vitae magistri nobis excitandi sunt."[23] In traditional philosophy, that "which presents itself of its own accord" is the evidence of the last principles; starting from this evidence being is determined independently of temporal and local relations; Guarino turns this process on its head. Evidence is now taken to be the "perceptibility" (*Anschaulichkeit*) of the single case, through which we immediately discover whether the bearing of witness has responded to—or missed—the appeal of the non-deducible and unfathomable. It is this "evidence" which evokes admiration.

There are two elements in the example: the "contemplatio" and the "ad-miratio." Guarino states that when reading Sallust we are "enflamed" by his images and spurred into action: "qui, ut apud Crispum lectitas, 'cum maiorum imagines intuerentur vehementissime animum ad virtutem accendi ferebant.' "[24] Through the use of example as "testimony" (as derived from the "doctrina litterarum") the difficulty in applying abstract norms to single cases is overcome. The distinction between abstract thinking and concrete acting, between true and good becomes, therefore, untenable. The "doctrina exemplorum" demands not a rational but an imaginative language which, as such, affects the passions and induces imitation: "suarum imitatione virtutum restituas crebramque illius recordationem pie amabiliterque conserves."[25]

Since the demands to which we must respond are always new, imitation cannot be considered a repetition of a previously performed action. Such an understanding of "imitatio" would fail to recognize the original horizon in the domain of which only the distinct meanings of being can appear. Therefore, it is not a matter of repeating a single case as such. Every example is evidence of a response to an appeal which always exists and forces itself upon us in ever new forms. It is in this sense that we have to understand Guarino's confession that in every action performed by him he is conscious "ut ubi sum ibi non sim, ubi non sum ibi sit animus meus."[26]

And thus arises the primacy of the "litterae": the "contemplatio" and the corresponding "admiratio" which are evoked have as their object not an abstract, unhistorical reality but the historical being disclosing itself in the "here" and "now." History will disclose the proper "text" in view of the different meanings of being: "Historia earum rerum et temporum descriptio est, quae nostra vidit aut videre potuit aetas." Guarino insists on this point and refers to the etymology of "historia": " Ἱστορεῖν (videre) Graeci dicunt et ἱστορίαν (spectaculum)."[27]

History is the stage and the "spectaculum" not only of the demands made on humans, but also of their victories and defeats with regard to these demands. History is nothing but a "sighting," a "showpiece," a spectacle of the hidden power through the commands of which the meaning of being manifests itself. "Historical accounts surpass any image and statue because they give us spiritual and moral examples; their voices ring over all the lands and the seas and they are found everywhere" [imaginem statuamque praecellunt . . . illi vero animos etiam effingunt et mores . . . illi voce sua terras implent et maria . . . illi per universum terrarum orbem facile pervagantur disseminarique valent].[28] Time is an essential element of history, for through time all that crowds in upon humans, including their due "re-sponsibility," manifests itself: "ne tempus ipsum iners ac desidiosum abire sinam."[29] Therefore: "ingentes historiarum scriptoribus habendae sunt gratiae, quod eorum labore tanta communi mortalium vitae utilitates pepererunt."

In order to be objective and historical, "contemplatio" must avoid any passion that might obscure the recognition of the demands experienced "here" and "now": ". . . (libera) sit mens ullis affectionibus . . ., at adeo libera ut nec res adversas enuntiare formides nec vera tacendo speres nec adversariorum profligatione gaudio effundere."[30]

If we acknowledge that the meaning of the real manifests itself in situations, the recourse to history must be interpreted as relating to these witnesses, which have opened up this specifically different understanding of being. Here we leave the ideal of a philosophy which takes shelter behind its abstract considerations. While discussing his translation into Latin of Plutarch's *Life of Themistocles*, Guarino maintains that through the life of this man the differences between the times, the changes in human affairs, the fortunes and vicissitudes of life, the events and the duplicity of their meaning, admiration as well as joy and anxiety become openly visible [Accedit . . . in hoc homine temporum varietas, rerum humanarum permutatio, fortunarum vicissitudines, ancipites variique casus, admiratio metus spes laetitia maeror].[31] By comparing our life with the demands which crowd in upon humans in varying situations, and with the varying responses to these demands, we are enabled to educate ourselves (*se componere*), to take a specific stand (*se instituere*), and to live with others [ut prudentiae in decernendo, facilitatis in audiendo, . . . comitatis et gravitatis in convivendo].[32]

History also implies "recte vivendi normam comparari cognosceres";[33] history takes on the task originally attributed to rational philosophy; history makes the spirit of the time visible. After quoting a passage from Vergil's *Aeneid* (IV, 336: "dum memor ipse mei, dum spiritus hos regit artus"), Guarino continues: ". . . quarum si non ipse splendor alliciat, utilitas tamen, dum hoc saeculo (spiritus hos reget artus), invitet."[34]

This engenders the necessity of recognizing the importance of praxis, of action. Guarino reminds us that someone who excels in the study of the liberal arts should have learned that it is contrary to his duties to be deterred from action: "liberalium artium studio ab rebus gerendis abduci contra officium est."[35] Guarino claims that neither peace nor repose but action is the prerogative of mortals: "Mortales enim ad aliquid semper agendum, non ad quietem non ad otium non ad standum."[36] But what are the "virtutes?" Guarino enumerates: *fides, integritas, diligentia, pietas*, and so on; and he points out that they are laudable only when put into practice [laus omnis in actione locuta est]. Guarino puts it thus: a "gymnasium" has been prepared for humans [tibi parata quaedam est palaestra], and history is the stage on which man conducts his own experiment [in qua . . . praestabis experimentum].[37] By studying history man elevates himself to the divine.[38]

In a letter Guarino mentions the criterion according to which the "virtutes" have to be chosen: they must do justice to the demands of nature and of public opinion [manifesto naturae consensu et innato cunctis iudicio]. It is nature which "forces" and "guides" us (*coget, ducet*) and we are, therefore, concerned with a realization of the "virtutes" in actual human society [in hominum consociatione et communitate versetur].[39] And again, in relation to Cicero, he identifies nature with Minerva: "Nihil egregie aut bene fieri potest (invita Minerva, hoc est adversante et repugnante natura); paululum sane contra natura rudes et ineptos doctrina prodest."[40]

To sum up: the "litterae" lead to the experience of the historical and this experience to a "se componere," "se formare," "se constituere": "non modo ad legendum sed etiam ad se componendum formandum instituendum."[41] The "being-there" learns through the "contemplatio" and the "admiratio." The pedagogy of Guarino works through "indications" and not through rational "proofs." It is said of a personality distinguished by his great caution that he not only recognizes the present situation [non modo praesentia intelligebat], but, like a prophet, has insight into the future [ventura prospiciebat].[42]

The original faculty basic to Guarino's pedagogy is not reason but "ingenium": "Qua in re tuo ingenio virtutique gratulor"[43]; "non autem rudis . . . ingenii, sed adeo politi et divini, ut, cum ingenium laudem, sapientiam etiam admirer colam venerer et observem."[44] Ingenium has been given to man so that he may have control of the "copia verborum" in respect of a variety of situations in which he finds himself: "deus nanque . . . tantam ingenii facultatem . . . suo infudit oratori."[45] If "de-monstrating" is in the realm of rational activity, "in-dicating" is the activity of the ingenium. Not ontology but the "litterae" as "optimarum disciplinae" form the basis for teaching and the preconditions for learning: "Hoc tempore pretiosissimos animi tui thesauros depromes, quos litterarum studiis et optimarum artium disciplinis . . . ab ineunte aetate comparasti."[46]

4

The Relationship between Theory and Praxis: Cristoforo Landino (1424–1498) and Coluccio Salutati (1331–1406)

Another burning problem which deeply occupied the Humanists is the relationship between theory and praxis and the question of their precedence. Here we can only allude to the problem. For the purpose of the present discussion, our interest is directed towards this question: Did the Humanists debate and resolve the problem by having recourse to the "litterae," or to a purely rational dispute?

As long as philosophy—according to the traditional ontological understanding—is concerned with the rational definition of being (that is, with "theory"), being appears to be "at the disposal" of every human action (or praxis) precisely because of its abstract determination (this is, detached from the "here" and "now"). For its own legitimization, praxis is therefore forced to fall back upon general concepts of theory. Exactly at this point a problem arises: how is the transition from the universal abstract to the concrete made. Aristotelian philosophy—and the medieval thinking which refers to it—has, for its own part, fallen back upon the theory of "prudentia," which we cannot deal with here. We have to deal with Humanism and how it solved this problem. We shall refer to two examples.

Cristoforo Landino in his *Disputationes Camaldulenses* refers to the "litterae" in solving the problem. On the other hand (and in accordance with traditional thinking), Coluccio Salutati, in *De nobilitate legum et medicinae* points to rational causal thinking, and, referring to Cicero, incorporates—in a rather arbitrary fashion—the arguments of the Romans into the sphere of Christian thinking.

Landino's *Disputationes Camaldulenses*[47] consists of four books. The first two books contain a theoretical discussion of the preeminence of theory over praxis; the other two treat the same problem with the help of an interpretation of Vergil's *Aeneid*. Critics have often debated the question of the relation between these two parts of the book, albeit from a purely speculative point of view. What is the meaning of the sudden reference to the metaphysical interpretation of a text?

The first book of the *Disputationes* offers a purely theoretical discussion between L. B. Alberti as the representative of traditional platonizing thought, and the young Lorenzo de Medici, the representative of praxis. Here, too, we have to limit ourselves to a brief outline. The basic thesis in Alberti's platonizing metaphysics is as follows: Praxis can be understood only as the execution of an eternal theory which is firmly based in itself. It concerns itself with referring the single case back to the realm of the universal, the temporal to the sphere of the eternal, history to the frame of the non-historical and everlasting. As our spirit—through which alone we are human beings—does not find fulfillment in transient actions but in intransient cognition, which represents that final goal toward which everything tends, and which is the target of all activity and aspiration, who would not then recognize the fact that a contemplative life is far nobler? [Verum cum mens nostra, qua sola homines sumus, non mortali actione, sed immortali cognitione perficiatur, in qua ultimum illud, quo omnia referuntur cuiusque causa omnia fiunt, ipsum autem propter se expetitur, collocatum sit, quis non viderit speculationem esse longe anteponendam?][48]

Lorenzo de Medici opposes this thesis and stresses the importance of praxis: It is impossible to separate the soul from the body and, therefore, theory from praxis, particularly because a human being is a social being. He defines action above all as "civilis actio": "Illud autem quis non videat ad concilia coetusque celebrandos et ad communem societatem conservandam nos parentem optimam naturam produxisse?"[49] If we live in a community which is protected by the walls of the city, and if we order our community within its compass according to its laws, we have to leave aside the mysteries of the divine entities and the secrets of nature, and direct all our attention to the actions which serve the establishment of the state and the family. If the sage focusses only on himself and has no relation to his fellow men, what then can his contribution to his community be? [sapiens otiosus oscitansque assit secumque et nullique admisceatur, neminem salutet, nullam neque privatim neque publice operam praestet]. Honors, trophies and columns of remembrance have meaning only as testimonies to social acts.[50]

In point of fact, Lorenzo de Medici's contribution is hardly a theoretical antithesis to Alberti's thesis. Landino treats the same problem again in the second book, not, however, on the basis of a theoretical discussion but through a quick survey of the treatment of that question in the history of philosophy. The fact that Landino deals with the problem in a historical exposition indicates his dissatisfaction with the antecedent debate.

As mentioned already, books three and four leave behind theoretical and historical considerations in order to fall back upon the "litterae." Our author does so in his discussion of the metaphorical interpretation of the *Aeneid.* At first glance, this might astonish the reader, who may wonder whether Landino has abandoned his search for a philosophical solution. Does Landino perhaps abstain from rational consideration in order to return to metaphorical thinking and speaking, solving in this way the problem which occupies the Humanists? Our author interprets the fate of Aeneas as a metaphor for the formation of a human being in order to answer the problem of the interrelations between theory and praxis.

A few hints must suffice: according to Landino's thesis, the story of Aeneas becomes a metaphor of one human existence which, in confrontation with varying situations (i.e., needs), slowly comes to an understanding of itself, and this happens in such a way that the intimate relationship between theory and praxis becomes obvious.

In order to understand the full extent of Landino's thesis we have to remember that the story of Aeneas' migration does not represent the experiences of any one person. His figure becomes a symbol of the historical continuity which exists between the Greek and the Roman world, that is, between two essential epochs in history. Aeneas is a "witness" of the historicity of occidental being. According to Landino, Vergil, through his poetic metaphor, has created for the Roman world what Homer has created for the Greek. The metaphor of the Aeneas story discloses the genesis of Roman social and political history without resorting to rational ontological and metaphysical considerations.

That Landino frequently resorts to the "ethical" in his interpretation of the "formation" of Aeneas should not be misunderstood: the moral judgment arises with the consciousness that the hero does not recognize in the demands of specific situations his own historic possibilities and his fate. "Therefore, Vergil adorns Aeneas with the most beautiful poetic inventions so that he, little by little enlightened by the admirable faculties, may finally attain that which is the *summum bonum* of man and attainable only to the sage after gradually being cleansed from most and the worst depravities."[51]

A human being is "purified" by facing experiences which force him to acknowledge the already existing order governing the historical situation in which he lives, or to develop a new order of an epoch. This presupposes that the human being has to act with regard to decisions which must be made "here" and "now." Persius had already said: "The spirit (*mens*) always finds itself at the cross-roads: if we are asked to proceed, it is unavoidable to go to the right or left."[52]

Vergil's poem is not, therefore, theoretical thinking in "literary disguise"; rather it wishes to disclose the inseparability of theory and praxis through the metaphor of the historicity of being. Landino takes the life of Aeneas in Troy to be a metaphor of the original human situation (*prima natura*). His innate faculties and passions are the preconditions of his later actions.[53] Accordingly, his departure from Troy represents his turning away from the immediate natural conditions[54] and, therefore, at the same time, the origin of his historicity.

Similarly, the section describing Aeneas' sea journey is essential.[55] It portrays the quest for adventure, the desire to put one's self to the test in face of the possibility of success or failure. The exile of Aeneas becomes the symbol of the situation of a man who has lost his immediately given and familiar environment and has to search now for what is most characteristically his "own" (*proprium*). The appeal for self-knowledge belongs to this process, symbolized in Aeneas' landfall at Delos and the prophecy of the oracle which takes place there;[56] just as the voyage to the seer Helenus (the symbol of the acting human being) may be interpreted as meaning that man can come to his own historicity only after having won clarity about his own desires and his capacity to overcome them.[57]

Landino emphasizes that Aeneas can reach Italy only after having achieved the various levels of different experiences. The encounter with the Cyclops[58] belongs to the time of "apprenticeship" and symbolizes the labors and errors of those who are chosen to make history; as such it is linked with the debate on the essence of tyranny. Aeneas' travel to Sicily[59] and his sojourn in Carthage[60] dramatize the dangers of actions whose principal tasks are not fully comprehended and therefore yield no insight. Only after his departure from Carthage and after landing in Italy,[61] where he creates an historic community, will Aeneas achieve unity of theory and praxis, i.e., the realization of his historic task. It is therefore the "litterae" and their metaphoric meaning which "indicate" and educate. Vergil's poem discloses the plight inherent in different situations and offers up a metaphoric interpretation of itself: it reveals a pedagogical understanding which is not derived from ontological metaphysics.

In order to fully understand the problematic from which we started, we should indicate here the difficulties which the Humanists had to face in their conflict with traditional thinking. We have already given the example of Petrarch's defense of poetry and his contention of its primacy in his speech on the Capitol and in his letter to Zoilo. Similarly, the contention of some medieval authors that poetry is the "integumentum" of truth proves that Petrarch is enmeshed in the difficulties of medieval thought. It seems, therefore, necessary to return to the vexatious efforts of the Humanists once again, in particular Salutati's book *De nobilitate legum et medicinae.* In this tract he leaves behind the problem of the word as the beginning of philosophy in order to return, against all expectations, to the traditional rational and metaphysical thinking. I say this because Salutati's thesis of the primacy of jurisprudence might make us think of finding a new evaluation of the historical character of reality. Salutati's *De nobilitate legum et medicinae*[62] defends his thesis of the primacy of jurisprudence against the trivium, i.e., the disciplines which deal with the *word,* as well as against the quadrivium, i.e., the disciplines which deal with *numbers* and *measures.*

Salutati's argument is as follows: The doctrine of the word, i.e., grammar, has *being* as its proper object [grammatica, licet a *rebus* que sunt essendi modus . . . mutuetur].[63] Logic in its turn has as its proper object the truth of being; finally, rhetoric must start from being if it wants to distinguish itself from sophistry. But all "things human" are the object of jurisprudence [*res humanas* tractant et dirigant].[64] For this reason the doctrines of the trivium — grammar, logic and rhetoric (i.e., of words) — have to submit to jurisprudence as the science of "things human": all three doctrines have to become "ministra sit legum."[65] Even rhetoric is defined as "civilis scientie magna et ampla pars."[66]

Salutati draws a similar conclusion with regard to the quadrivium. Its doctrines, too, become meaningful only with regard to "things human": the measuring of bodies, the numbers of the manifold of being, the order of musical tones, the celestial bodies [. . . cum omnia de quibus agitant propter hominem sint, ut philosophi volunt, imo creata fuerint, ut vult divinissima theologia, legibus que hominibus imperant et humanos actus dirigunt ne supra finem suum se extollant].[67]

Thus the problem of jurisprudence turns out to be of principal importance: Salutati derives the term "jus" (the law) from "juvare" (to be useful), or from Jove, the god who founds and rules everything: "Ius igitur,
quod a iuvando dicitur vel forsitan a Iove, qui primus leges constituit"[68]
"Lex" is that which "binds" all human actions and by doing so makes human social order possible by supplying the "ratio actuum humanorum."
"Ab eligendo igitur, et se ligando, tandemque legendo, lex dicta est, tamquam electa, ligans atque legenda.[69] From this we could take jurisprudence as a doctrine which supports and binds human action, and, therefore,
as a renewed affirmation of the historicity of human beings. But this would
be a fundamental misunderstanding of Salutati's thought.

For Salutati, man is God's image, and for that reason there must exist
a "similitudo" between the divine and the human [humana similitudinem
habeant divinorum].[70] Accordingly, the laws are regarded as "vestigium,"
as a vestige, or as a "promulgatio" of the divine. In *De nobilitate legum
et medicinae* Salutati identifies the "vestige" of the divine with the *rational*: "ad illud rationis examen sufficit."[71] Everything remaining outside the
rational process is of inferior value: "nobilius est opus aliquod ratione sola
perfici, quam cum ultra rationem oportet aliquid extrinsecus adhiberi."[72]
Thus Salutati returns to the traditional causal mode of thinking in order
to justify the laws and their primacy. Everything that is governed by something else [quod ab alio gubernatur] must have its original reason in it
[rationem habeat gubernantis]; otherwise there would be no transition between them, no "transitio" [alias enim in eum talis operatio non tran-
siret].[73] It is obvious that in saying this Salutati adheres to the traditional
scheme of rational thinking.

Ever since the Platonic interpretation of the thoughts of Socrates, philosophizing has been identified with the rational and causal mode of thinking.
Every phenomenon has a cause, and an understanding of being is gained
through the rational clarification of this cause. In practice, however, this
model of thinking does not lead to an "elucidation" of the phenomenon.
Any cause is a "not yet" of the effect resulting from it, and at the same
time it is a "no longer" as soon as the effect has occurred. The causal
relationship between cause and effect supplies only the temporal sequence
of the moments of becoming, but never their meaning. Meaning cannot
be derived from the temporal sequence. A sound as effect of a cause (stroke)
can have the meaning of a call, of warning, of fright, or of joy. The model
of causal thinking is obviously completely abstract in its structure. It is

exactly the abstractness which makes it possible for Salutati to identify successfully the "nature" of which Cicero speaks arbitrarily with the "divine" of Christian thinking; he then takes this arbitrary identification as the basis for jurisprudence.

Salutati supports his own thesis about the divine foundation of jurisprudence with a passage in Cicero's *Tusculanae* (3.1.2) and another one in *De legibus* (1.6.18).[74] In the *Tusculanae* Cicero argues as follows: if nature had created us in a fashion which enabled us to understand immediately the meaning of being, there would be no need for slow and difficult investigation. Nature has also produced the small shining fire, the light of which is soon darkened by bad mores and wrong opinions. For Cicero, "nature" is the basis of the laws. A passage in *De legibus* (1.12.33) to which Salutati refers maintains that the law pronounces "naturally" what must or must not be done. [Lex est ratio summa insita in natura que iubet ea que facienda sunt prohibetque contraria].[75] The eternal divine reason of Christian metaphysics, of which Salutati speaks, is most certainly not the reason of nature to which Cicero refers, nor is it possible on the basis of causal thinking to decide whether nature or god is the basis for jurisprudence.

With *De nobilitate* we are again completely removed from the Humanist tradition which we have emphasized so far. We have left the problem of the word behind and have fallen back onto causal thinking and onto the rational definition of the foundation of the "res humanae." For this reason the problem becomes even more pressing: where can we find the "ratio vivendi?" Can it be found on the basis of an ontology in accordance with the traditional scheme, or on the basis of a philosophy which starts with the word and discloses the sphere in which human beings respond to demands of changing situations? In the latter case the word is no longer understood as an assimilation to being defined rationally, but as an answer to a question which forces itself upon us in concrete situations.

The humanist tradition, to which we have referred so far, inverts the traditional interpretation. The pedagogy of Guarino does not start from any ontology but from the "litterae." By interpreting a variety of texts we come to experience the appeal, on the basis of which the "being-there" realizes itself in history. Among those texts poetic and historical writings obtain preeminence. The poetic texts bear witness to a human being's responses through "transferences" to the demands made upon him; the historical texts give evidence of the different demands in respect to which being is disclosed in its ever-changing meanings.

CHAPTER FOUR

The Problem of "Ratio Vivendi"

1
"Necessitas" and "Ingenium"
in Juan Luis Vives (1492–1540)

UP TO NOW WE HAVE PURSUED THE FOLLOWING LINE OF THOUGHT: traditional occidental philosophy, which begins with Plato's interpretation of the thinking of Socrates, defines itself as metaphysics and, in particular, as the question of the essence of being. The whole of Platonic and Aristotelian thought aims to overcome the relativity and subjectivity in which being (things, the "res") appears to us: this philosophy stresses the dominant function of rational thought. From this follows the thesis that the objectivity of being can only be reached if the reasons of being are disclosed: the stating of reasons furnishes the ex-*planation* (Er-*klärung*) of being. By stating the genus and specific difference we arrive at a definition of beings. Through the rational process, philosophy as ontological metaphysics discovers the prime reason of being, and this is identified with God.

The precondition of this traditional thinking is that every being mediated to us through our senses has an essence which exists per se (οὐσία): the leading problem is the rational determination of the "res," as a function of which the word (verbum) can only receives its significance. However, it is the problem of being which has precedence, not the problem of the word. Ontology — that is, the determination of beings — is therefore the basis of language, and this implies the preeminence of the problem of the "res" over the problem of the "verbum."

We have already indicated how, in spite of the change in philosophical thinking from antiquity through the Middle Ages to modern thought, the exclusion of rhetoric and poetry from the field of scholarly thinking remains unchallenged. Only the fundamentally rational clarification of being is important; Descartes as well as Kant and Hegel belittle oratory as the art of persuasion and literature as merely "literary" expression.[1] Hegel emphasizes that the reasonable (*das Vernüftige*), which forms the nucleus of the real, is clothed in a colorful bark "which the *concept* must first penetrate"[2]; only when this is achieved do we arrive at philosophy. However, in Humanistic philosophy a reversal of this understanding occurs: we have already shown how the Humanist philologist experiences, through the interpretation of a text, the fact that the meaning of a word is not arrived at solely through a logical and abstract determination of the "res."

It is the intention of the interpreter (*Interpret*) to discover the individually differing significance of the words in their contexts. The Humanist tradition does not start from the problem of the logical determination of being, but from the problem of the word as the original domain in which the demand and the appeal (i.e., the existential needs) must be answered. The question of the essence of the demand of the existential needs is the starting point of the philosophy of Juan Luis Vives. His relationship to the Italian Humanists may be clarified by referring to a passage from his book *De disciplinis*: in this work he particularly mentions Leonardo Bruni (who is called "Aretino") and Poliziano: "Memoria patrum et avorum coeptum est in Italia revocari studium linguarum per discipulos Petri Ravennatis Latini, et Emmanuelis Chrysolorae Graeci, *inter quos maximi nominis fuere Leonardus Aretinus . . . Angelus Politianus.*"[3]

In his central treatise Vives declares openly that he will not start from the Sacred Scriptures so as not to mix theology and philosophy; instead, he will start from nature: "ideoque rationes attuli petitas *ex natura*, non e divinis oraculis, ne ex philosophia in theologiam transilirem."[4] We must, therefore, ask what Vives means by this reference to nature. Should we see this reference as a throwback of the traditional metaphysics of beings, perhaps indicating a break with the Humanist problematic?

Vives attributes to man a primal instinct for preservation which he relates to the concept of nature: "amor tuendi sui, quem illi indidit natura."[5] Yet man is distinguished from other living beings by the lack of much that is necessary for his own realization: "Animantes omnes naturae

benignitate, ac magisterio, satis esse ad tuendam vitam instructas vide-
mus . . . homo vero prodit in lucem hanc multarum rerum indigus."[6]

The "needs," the requirements attendant upon man always provide the
motivation to seek and find responses. Vives talks of the dominant "necessitas": ". . . homo . . . in tenebras est prolapsus, in quibus tamen ursit
atque extimulavit eum necessitas, perpetuo premens ut quaereret."[7]
Man—in the darkness in which he finds himself—is forced to find satisfaction for the needs he experiences; this is by no means a subjective or arbitrary process. Vives makes use of a metaphor in his explanation: human
endeavors resemble a search for pearls in oysters or precious jewels in
the rocks which hide them.[8] The "disciplinae" provide man with the objective and factual answers to the demands with which nature confronts
him. The original "invention" consists in such a response to a need.[9]

The sciences have no "formal" character; they receive their meaning
only when the demands with which nature confronts man are fulfilled: they
are otherwise vacuous, arbitrary, boring, unbearable, and without stimu-
lus: "si non stimulis quibusdam urgeretur, ac excitaretur, nihil fieri possit
illo squalidius aut horridius; primum necessitas acutissimum calcar
addidit.[10]

The power of the arts must therefore be equal to the power of nature:
only in the arts is man able to come to terms with nature. Only in the
arts does nature become apparent as an element of the human world: "ex
spectatione theatri huius naturae maxime capiuntur":[11] "omnia ad hominis *usum* condidisset."[12]

Clearly, the terminology of appeal and response, which we have used
here, is justified: they are the needs which urge man to "give a voice"
to things. Only through fulfilling our needs do we gain information about
the "code" with which we "read" reality.

2

The Ingenious Activity

What makes the realization of the "artes" possible is, according to Vives,
not the rational, abstract proving activity but the "discovering activity" of
the ingenium: "*Inventor artium et disciplinarum omnium est ingenium*, acu-
mine et solertia praeditum ac instructum, sed diligentia atque usu vehemen-

ter adjuvatur; nam per diligentiam et procedit longius, et plura ei se aperiunt quae prius erant abdita et occulta, non aliter quam navigantibus."[13] Vives declares that there is nothing more beautiful than caring for the ingenium (*cultus ingeniorum*): through it man both comes to himself and distinguishes himself from the animals: "disciplinae . . . qui nos a ferarum ritu et more separat, humanitati restituit."[14]

In order to make us fully aware of the significance of ingenious thinking it is important to remind ourselves of the Latin understanding of the term "ingenium." Even the etymology of the word "ingenium" (derived from *gignere*) points towards its relationship with the word nature (derived from *nasci*). In Vergil, as well as in Ovid and Statius, "ingenium" gains the meaning of a power which determines growth, existence and passing away, that is, the becoming of beings. In Vergil "ingenium" is spoken of as the "naturalis proprietas" of the soil.[15] Ovid mentions "ingenium" in connection with nature, insofar as nature creates something by itself which looks as though it were created by human art.[16] Statius, for his part, recognizes the effect of the ingenium in the external image of nature, e.g., in landscape.[17]

In the Latin tradition, "ingenium" is used concerning the behavior of animals in general and human activity. Vergil maintains that birds possess more ingenium than humans,[18] and he describes the ability, the talent and performance of man as ingenious;[19] so does Ovid.[20] In philosophy, ingenium leads to the vision which discovers what is hidden.[21] Ovid also maintains that the ingenium is comparable to a life-vein, which is fed by the spring of the Muses[22] in such a fashion that the ingenious vision has a sacred character.[23] Cicero describes the ingenium as an "archaic," that is, a primal, non-reducible, and dominant power: as such, ingenium lifts man above the habitual forms of thinking and feeling: "Magni autem est ingenii sevocare mentem a sensibus et cogitationem ab consuetudine abducere."[24] It unites man with the Divine and, therefore, enables him to recognize the laws of the universe which are an expression of the godhead.[25] Ingenium is the source of the "ars inveniendi," while ratio is the origin of the "ars judicandi."

In light of this tradition we may understand Vives' thesis of the ingenium as source of the "disciplinae." The ingenious power is sagacious[26], whereas ratio is the power of the slow process which orders deductively what has been discovered by the ingenium.[27] Elsewhere, Vives points out that alongside the ingenium we find the rational power of judgment, which through causal reasoning collects and justifies that which is manifold but not yet unified.[28] Again and again Vives distinguishes the discovering and disclosing activity of the ratio by explicitly using the terminology of "disclosing": ". . . illique inventores dicti, non quasi rem, quae non esset, fecissent ipsi, *sed detexissent, quae lateret*.[29]

From this Vives draws the conclusion that the ingenium discovers what the appeal of nature and the human response to this appeal have in common, case by case, "here" and "now." This "communality," the finding of which is the essence of the "disciplinae," cannot be gained through a rational, abstracting process. Acuteness (*agudeza*), which belongs inherently to ingenious discovering, is considered by Vives the insight which penetrates to the very depth of a problem. He states explicitly that a speech is acute if its words penetrate to the heart of the argument.[30] The ingenium is a power of nature[31]; from it are derived *diligentia,* conscientiousness, and attentiveness: "In diligentia sunt animi intentio, et quasi vigilia quaedam . . . cura, sedulitas, labor: inventor artium at disciplinarum omnium est ingenium."[32] They lead to satisfaction and to the admiration of what has been discovered.[33]

Vives speaks constantly of the demands made by nature: when they respond to these demands in the *artes,* humans elevate themselves to something higher.[34] When considering the sciences, Vives does not start from the thesis of the "natural light" (of reason) but from the ingenious activity which creates the "clearing": "adjuti *luce* quadum, velut duce viae . . . lux erat vis mentis et acumen, quo prospicerent quò eundum esset, et quà."[35] The ethical, economic, and political disciplines—as responses to nature—are dis-covered by the ingenium: without these responses man would neither live nor lead a human existence. His life would be a feral life.[36]

Again we should note the basic thesis of Vives: man has to respond to that which Vives defines as "nature"; he does so through the "inventio": "Prima rerum inventio necessitati succurrit."[37] "Inventio," in its turn, originates from the activity of the ingenium: "God has given Man that instrument with the help of which he can progress: it is the living and autonomous acumen of the ingenium; it is the origin of all human discoveries."[38] To it also belongs language: ". . . unde confecta est verborum, sermonis, linguarum tanta varietas, et copia."[39] Vives therefore maintains: ". . . vocum significatio, hoc est, notatio, *animum spectat, non res*."[40]

Herein lies also the reason why it is not the rational, abstract language which is important, but the historical: "observata sunt verba singula, tum phrases ac loquendi modi, ut apti essent usui, hoc est, ut consensu essent publico notati, quod est velut *communis monetae signum.*"[41] Vives therefore rejects abstract meanings and general and universal definitions of words: "Significare vero non simpliciter sumendum est, aut universaliter, sed semper respectu et ratione alicuius."[42]

If humans take their place within the framework of ever new "situations," language–ingenious, rhetorical language, not a rational language which abstracts from the given situation–is the primal condition of human togetherness. Vives maintains in his *De ratione dicendi* that language is the "consociationis vinculum"[43] and, in a different work, that language is the "helm" of society.[44] If ingenious thinking and speaking are possible only within the framework of concrete situations, we can infer the importance of the historical character of the word. In and through the word a response is made to the appeal and the address.

If our interpretation of Vives stresses above all the ingenious activity as the main content of his philosophy, it is necessary to avoid a simple error: we could be tempted to overlook the connection existing between Vives and Humanism. Vives and Humanism (insofar as it takes the problem of the word as its starting point) put heavy emphasis on the question of the essence and structure of the appeal do which man responds in the word. Only in regard to this appeal to the word and the activity of the ingenium assume their functions. If taken differently, the theory of the ingenium would become a plain anthropological doctrine, as in the case of *Examen de ingenios para las sciencias* (1575) by Juan Huarte (1529–1588), which Lessing translated into German.

According to Vives, man appears as the creator of his world, but only insofar as he responds to the questions arising from the "necessitates." Man is not the lonely principal actor, the arbitrary shaper of his history; he is the "re-sponsible" vis-à-vis the experienced "re-quirements." Vives gives us not an anthropology but a new way of presenting the metaphysical problem. His way of looking at the problem pinpoints the essential difference between the task of rationally defining being–in accordance with the scheme of traditional thinking–and the task of discovering the meaning of beings as the response to differing "necessitates" which are urges upon the "being-there."

Such an understanding is intimately linked to the problem of the appeal, which in its originality and non-deductibility–and, therefore, from a rational point of view, its unfathomable character–can be experienced only in its disclosure in history. The Humanists return time and again to this thesis. The ingenious word is the primal form through which we respond to the "necessitates" which impose themselves upon us in various situations. The close relationship between the "necessitates" and the "ingenium" is established in the consciousness in such a fashion that the ingenious activity in no way "proves" anything in responding to the urging compulsion; rather, it only "indicates" through disclosure the "here" and "now" of the ruling situation. For this reason, the concept of "experience" (as well as the concept of a pure "rhetorical language") must be understood as expressing a confrontation with the compulsion which manifests itself in the situation: "ornatius dicendi, et acutius inveniendi, *ex necessitate* fluxit."[45]

In Vives, as in other authors to whom we have referred, there already emerge two essential theses which Vico—three centuries later—will develop to their fullest philosophical import. First, the dis-closing of being is not based on a rational ontology of beings but on the urgency of the metaphoric poetic word: Vico will maintain the originality of the "universale fantastico." The second thesis deals with the self-disclosing of being in its historicity, especially through stressing the identity of "verum" and "factum"; that is, the responding activity is guided primarily by the "fantastic" and "ingenious" and not by rational universals. However, whereas Vico discovers the activity of the ingenium primarily in the poetic, metaphoric word, Vives had sought and identified it in the different "disciplinae." Being as the disclosure of a necessity (which Vico calls "divine") is identified by the same Vico with the realization of a "pro-vidence"; and this "pro-vidence," the disclosure of the past, present and future, makes insight into the meaning of history first possible.

3
"Voluptas" or "Honestas" as "Ratio Vivendi":
Lorenzo Valla (1405–1457)

The problems with which we are confronted at this point of our investigation are as follows: if the significance of the "res" presents itself differently in accordance with varying situations, what then is the essence and the structure of the appeal in the framework of which the meaning of the "res" becomes clear? What is the "indicating" – not the rationally "proving" – primal semantic sign that the unfathomable appeal has been fulfilled? What relationship exists in this problematic between the "res" and "verbum?" We deal here with the problem of being neither as subject nor as object, but with the problem of the clarification of the unfathomable appeal in which "being-there" discovers itself. In order to discuss this question we start not from Lorenzo Valla's *Disputationes dialecticae,* which contains a discussion about traditional logic and ontology, but from his treatise *De vero falsoque bono* (*De voluptate*). The problem of "voluptas" was itself topical during the period of Humanism: it is also a theme in Francesco Filelfo (1398–1481), in Cosma Raimondi (fifteenth century), and in Leonardo Bruni's translation of Aristotle's *Ethics.*

For Valla, the primal semantic sign through which the interpretation of the significance of being issues is "voluptas" (Lust), pleasure. The central problem of interpretation which faces us is a more precise exegesis of the term. To discover the significance of the term "voluptas" and the reason why Valla chooses it as the staring point of his philosophizing, we can refer to Valla's own remarks. When writing his first version of *De voluptate* in 1429–30, the young Valla discusses how much the title of his treatise means to him:

> If any one of my friends were to feel repulsed by the title of my treatise and the persistence with which I am attached to it, and if he were perhaps to ask me what strange fancy urges me to write about it – the pleasure to which I was never devoted and to which it should not appear that I had any inclination towards – I will and ought to answer in honesty and friendship any one who asks this question . . . I have preferred to give my treatise the title "On Pleasure" *because of the nature of the flexible and non-rigid but open term* [molli quodam et non individioso nomine].

And Valla adds immediately: "Indeed, I say and insist and repeat that there is no other good but pleasure."[46] In fact, it turns out that the composition of *De voluptate* results from the constant change in meaning of the term "pleasure."

Valla points out explicitly that the meaning of the term "voluptas" is equivalent to that of the Greek ἡδονή: "Pleasure is a good which is always sought, and it consists in the enjoyment of body and soul . . . what the

Greeks call 'hedone' . . . And as Cicero says: no other term than 'voluptas' would express in Latin what the Greeks mean by 'hedone.' "[47] Yet right from the beginning the meaning of voluptas is not given by a "final" definition; the point is to ask oneself repeatedly what this word means. The task is to investigate the "mollitia," the changeability of this term.

The starting point of Valla's discussion is the fact that "voluptas" is identified with the Epicurean interpretation of the term, with the pleasure of the senses, and, as such, acclaimed: "voluptas" as an indicating sign pointing to the primal demands of life as unfathomable reality. "Nature has urged nothing so much on the genus of living beings as the necessity to save themselves and to avoid that which is detrimental to them. For what protects life more than pleasure?"[48] Here we have the precondition of Valla's theoretical discussion.

The critique of the Epicurean exegesis of pleasure (Lust) is best represented by Stoicism, for which the temptation of the passions by the senses and the resulting confusion and obscurity are evil itself. Therefore, pleasure contains two opposing meanings. Which is the correct one? For the Stoic, everything which humans experience through their senses lies in the realm of the dark and the relative, which man must strive to leave: "Natura enim excecavit mentes hominum que illuminare debebat ne lucem sapientie contemplentur."[49] "Voluptas" is the absolute negative, the expression of nature as the realm of becoming; man must raise himself from this realm through the "ratio," in order to arrive, through abstraction, at pure, eternal, and lasting being.

From this premise arise the constant complaints of Stoicism against nature and the temptation of pleasure, as well as the question of why nature has treated man niggardly in contrast to all other living beings. "Ratio," which is the essence of man, is completely impotent against the passions and appetites.

It is generally accepted that Nature spontaneously intends that which is good and spontaneously avoids that which is bad. This hold true for animals who have received nothing better than their bodies: they flee hunger, thirst, cold, heat and death. . . . For us human beings who are characterized by the possession of reason—through which we are related to the eternal gods—"honestas" is the eternal good. But if that is the order of things, why then do we flee "honestas" and turn to its opposite, vice?[50]

This starting point of Valla's philosophizing goes far beyond the borders of the debate between Stoicism and Epicureanism. In the whole of traditional philosophy, insofar it is rooted in the problematic of Platonism or Aristotelianism, everything that is mediated through the senses is thought obscure and relative, and must be opposed by rational activity. Traditional philosophy leads to the concept of "honestas" as the basic attitude of man, who is deceived by the senses and passions. "Honestas" results from the realization of the four cardinal virtues: "justitia," "fortitudo," "temperantia," and "prudentia." Basing himself on Cicero's treatise *De finibus*, Valla maintains: "Ille autem quatuorque virtutes appellantur, quas vos honestatis vocabulo coinquinatis."[51] Valla determines "virtus" as "ratio vivendi": "in virtutibus, quibus constat omnis ratio vivendi."[52] "Honestas," the quintessence of the cardinal virtues, embodies "human" life and that which gives justification for action. His thesis is: "In nobis, *qui sumus rationis compotes* et per hanc cum diis immortalibus socii, *honestas* unicum bonum est, vitiositas malum."[53] This definition corresponds to Cicero's: "Honestum igitur id intelligimus, quod tale est, ut detracta omni utilitate, sine ullis praemiis fructibusve per se ipsum possit iure laudari."[54]

The original realm of "honestas" is the domain of rationality: the world of ideas. The Stoics and Platonists complain against "voluptas" as "ratio vivendi" in order to affirm the power of the "ratio" and to escape from "niggardly" Nature. The place of ideas – to which we come through the rational overcoming of the sensual – is the place of the trans-sensual, the realm of hyperuranion, of contemplation. The method by which we arrive there is rational thinking – as accomplished by Plato or Aristotle. Valla will therefore examine the understanding which is the essence of the thinking of antiquity. Valla chooses the concept of "voluptas" and its opposite, "honestas," in order to debate traditional metaphysics.

However, the problem which Valla takes as his starting point in *De voluptate* is not only or not so much the debate between Epicureanism and Stoicism, as most critics seem to think (and how could we be interested today in such a discussion, except from a historical point of view?), but rather an attack on traditional metaphysics and on Christian thought insofar as they are anchored in Platonism and Aristotelianism. Does traditional rationalistic philosophy, with its concept of "honestas," provide a "ratio vivendi?" Does a reality correspond to that word?

4

Critique of the Ancient Concept of "Honestas"

In his dialogue *Philebos* Plato takes up the problem of ἡδονή and points out that pleasure arises when a deficiency e.g., pain (λύπη), is eliminated. He emphasizes in this context that the living being originally has to have a sign – an idea – within itself in order to recognize pleasure as such. If that were not the case, how could a living being which never before has experienced pleasure feel an urge toward it and acclaim that which is full of pleasure as such? From this Plato draws the conclusion: there must exist per se a world of ideas, a hyperuranic dimension to which we all aspire and in which we first attain the original reality.

Epicureanism opposes the thesis of an *a priori* idea of pleasure and of a transcendent world. As a living being, man belongs to "nature," that is, to the domain of the phyein, which is interpreted as the original creation, existence and disappearance of being. "Voluptas" is the sign which always appears when the appeal of nature in form of sensual needs is responded to. Traditional Platonizing philosophy identifies "voluptas" with the negative and the disturbing, which has to be overcome by "ratio." If, however, as we shall see, the whole intention of *De voluptate* is the refutation of the traditional Platonizing and Aristotelizing understanding of "virtus" as the "ratio vivendi," how then can we understand the essence of "voluptas?"

The most surprising aspect of Valla's treatise is that the reader expects a systematic, tract-like investigation of "voluptas" that would correspond to the model of traditional philosophy. Instead, right from the beginning, he finds a discussion of the meaning of the two words "voluptas" and "honestas." Which "res" responds to them? An Epicurean, a rational Platonizing, or a third meaning: which will Valla discover?

For Valla the word is no *trait d'union* between man as subject and the being with which he is confronted as object. Such a procedure would imply that philosophical research – in accordance with traditional understanding and method – begins from a rational determination of being. Instead, in and through the word, in and through language – as a response to the original appeal – Valla asks this question: what corresponds to the concepts "voluptas" and "honestas" as the two fundamental forms of the ancient "ratio vivendi," or, rather, which "res" stands behind the word; or are the concepts "empty?" We are, therefore, witness to a debate of principle, whether of Epicureanism or Platonism, which begins from the problem of the word, and not from a rational determination of the "res."

When using this method we abandon the ontological perspective of traditional speculation. Because Valla knows this, he speaks of a new method: "novas quandam inivi rationes." In order to understand the full impact of his critique of "honestas," we must keep in mind the fact that in antiquity men sacrificed themselves for the sake of "honestas," which, they believed, provided a meaning and a reason for their actions, institutions and their politics, and a means of distinguishing themselves from the world of the "barbarians." We have to consider how topical and unheard of – particularly in the age of Humanism – Valla's task is, for it is precisely at this time that antiquity is revalued.

The changing meaning of "voluptas" in the course of Valla's treatise – first in accordance with Epicureanism, then with Stoic Platonism and, finally, in Valla's own attempt to interpret it in a completely new way – makes us understand why he determines the concept as a "molle et non invidiosum nomen."

The first critique to which Valla subjects the concept of "honestas" is intended to show that the virtues, which are the preconditions of "honestas," are in fact – according to Epicureanism – only *masks*, behind which 'voluptas' appears as the only concrete "res." A "demasking" is therefore necessary. "We shall prove that the hunters of wisdom [the Stoics] do not desire any virtue but only shadows of virtues, no 'honestas' but only 'vanity,' no sense of duty, but only injustice, no wisdom, but 'insanity.' "[55]

Valla places the weight of his critique of "honestas" on an analysis of "fortitudo."[56] Man fights, sheds his blood and sacrifices his life. "Fortiter, viri voluptatemne calculis subductis proelium ineunt, sanguinem pro patria profundunt, an quondam animi ardore atque impetu concitati."[57] Tradition maintains that "fortitudo" is one of the cardinal virtues through which we gain tranquility, calmness, and serenity; through it we are able to master the obscuring passions. "Fortitudo" should therefore represent the reflection of an "ideal," transcendent reality for which man should sacrifice himself: it pretends to disclose the human world in all its dignity; it is the reflection of a "suprahistoric" reality.

In accordance with the objection of the Epicureans, Valla negates this thesis: No one realizes "fortitudo" for its own sake; humans realize this virtue either through their pleasure in the affirmation of life, through their pleasure in overcoming difficulties, or through their pleasure in security and dignity. "Honestas" is an "empty" word which hides a "res," i.e., the "voluptas"; there is nothing transcendent or extra-historical about the term.

The same is true for "justitia": it regulates the instincts of humans in order to maintain the sensitive equilibrium of society, so that we may live in it without disturbance; therefore it is for the sake of "voluptas." "Justitia" is only the expression of an attitude which the individual needs in order to assert his own life within the community. "Prudentia," yet another cardinal virtue, Valla refers back to "commoda prospicere, incommoda vitare"; "continentia" is interpreted "ut una aliqua obligatione contineas quo pluribus et maioribus fruaris"; the previously mentioned "justitia" is an attitude which "tibi inter mortales benevolentiam, gratiam commodaque concilies."[58]

Valla draws from this "demasking" (which he pursues further) the conclusion that it is "voluptas" which is "domina inter ancillas." "Nihil est generi animantium tam a natura tributum quam ut se, vitam corpusque tueatur declinetque ea que nocitura videantur. Nunc autem quid magis vitam conservat quam voluptas, ut in gustu, visu, auditu, odoratu, tactu, sine quibus vivere non possumus, sine honestate possumus."[59] On the basis of this insight Valla is able to make his negative judgment about "honestas": ". . . vocabulum ipsum nihil ad rem pertinere."[60] And therefore the ever recurring question arises again: what is "voluptas?" Only a self-assertion of the living? Is it only Epicureanim versus Platonism?

Up to this point we have tried to show that behind the "verbum" "honestas"—as concrete "res"—there is only "voluptas," albeit masked. But now Valla proceeds to a second critique of "honestas." Even while masked, "honestas" aims at procuring enjoyment. But it does not even reach that goal, and thus the action which responds to it proves to be pure madness, "dementia."

The categories of "usus" and "fruitio" which appear in Valla's discussion lead to yet a further level in the critique of the concept of "honestas." The concept of "utilitas" is fundamental to classical ethics: for the Peripatetic philosopher "utilitas" is the realization of the common good; for the Stoic it is the realization of the self in harmony with the cosmos, whereas the Epicurean develops the concept on the basis of personal interests. In other words, the second critique of "honestas" presupposes that Valla sets out from the problem of the appeal in which things and being appear in their "usefulness." We are thus not dealing with a rational determination of being: "usus" and "fruitio" belong to "voluptas" as signs of the response to needs.

To take an example: Valla derives "honestas" from "honorare"—to honor—and from the resulting honor (fame). Honor is one of the most desired forms of recognition—it is achieved through our own self-affirmation; and for this man sacrifices himself. In other words, "voluptas" is supposed to represent the "utilitas," the reward for virtuous actions. Valla's thesis that, with respect to honor and fame, "honestas" does not lead to "voluptas" and therefore constitutes madness, is supported by the following argument: "One time follows the other and each cares only for itself [pro se queque sollicita est]. No one knows what the preceding generations have created and no one makes an effort to preserve the knowledge thereof; and even if this should happen, then one will either judge the past wrongly or have no admiration for it."[61] In the dust of forgetfulness the striving for honor dissolves into a ridiculous illusion: "I call you, Gods of the Heavens, of the Earth, of the Sea: if I had a choice, I would not care more for the honor of a Romulus or Numa Pompilius than for any shepherd whom nobody remembers."[62]

Should one die for the fatherland—like Regulus—not for the sake of honor but in order to preserve the liberty and existence of the fatherland? The dead will not be able to enjoy it. But how then is "honestas" to be established as the "ratio vivendi?" Valla leads his Epicurean to ask why, in the classical tradition, the individual takes upon himself labors, damages, dangers, and finally death? Or which reward, which goal has been proposed to him? The Stoic will suggest the reward of honor, the realization of virtue, or the freedom of the fatherland with all the benefits and joys which are connected to it. However, those who have contributed to these rewards are the ones who—because of their death—are barred from participating in them. "O stupid Codrus, Curtius, Decius, and Regulus and similar strong men, what did you achieve with your virtue? To die in order to be robbed of the rewards resulting from your courage and labor?"[63] The Platonizing Stoic will say that the sacrifices for "honestas" have to be made "per se," that is, when we do not receive any reward, when we act purely for the sake of "honestas," for "honestas" does not ask for any better reward than our own action" [nec premium sibi honestas aliquod postulat: ipsi sibi premium est optimum]. To this Valla replies with the argument of the Epicureans:

"I have never heard more absurd advice. What is it supposed to mean that "honestas" per se is a reward? I have to act with courage: why?

For the sake of "honestas!" But what is "honestas?" Precisely to act with courage! This seems to me a play on words, not an analysis. That sentence means only: I shall act courageously – in order to act with courage I shall go to meet death – in order to die. Is this a reward? It is far better to recognize that "honestas" is an empty illusion, something imagined which does not lead to any result."[64]

The third critique to which Valla subjects traditional metaphysics is also the most decisive, for it leads to a critique of the traditional rational method of philosophizing. Again and again Valla proves, through his representative of Epicureanism, that "honestas" is either based on "voluptas" (and only when a "res" corresponds to the "verbum") or, if this is not the case, the "verbum" is revealed as "empty." It must be emphasized that up to this point the original meaning of the term "voluptas" still remains wide open: Valla has so far only demonstrated that the "ratio vivendi" of antiquity produced by Platonism and Aristotelism is "vacuous." Therefore, the question still remains unanswered: must "voluptas" be understood an an affirmation of life along the lines of the Epicurean interterpretation?

The third critique which Valla levels at "honestas" proceeds from the following question: by what method does traditional philosophy try to define "honestas" or the corresponding virtues which lead to it? Traditional philosophy proceeds by means of a rational process, as demonstrated in an exemplary fashion by Aristotle in his *Nicomachean Ethics*.[65]

Is this method valid? The traditional definitions determine the virtues only in their universality, never with respect to the concrete situation in the midst of which man must act. "Fortitudo" (courage) can be defined as "temeritas" (temerity) when the fighter battles on knowing that it is useless.[66] Therefore, what in one situation – at a distinct place and at a distinct time – appears to be a virtue is patently a vice in a changed situation. Therefore, Valla arrives at the following objection: "Why, then, are two different things [i.e., "fortitudo" and "temeritas"] compressed into one?"[67] Valla continues: "Why is one word divided into two meanings in a fashion which is not permitted by their nature?"[68] Only with respect to the concrete situation can something be determined, not "per se" and in an abstract manner. The consequence which Valla draws from this is decisive: it is important that all being be given its name *in response to its time*: "Quin tribuis sua quibusque nomina, sua tempora, suas vices? *Nec enim semper iidem sumus* immo nec esse possumus."[70] Things and their meanings do

not come about simultaneously, but successively. It is therefore errone-
ous to press together what time has separated: "absurdum sit . . . que tempus distraxerit ea sub unum tempus velle coniungere."[70]

The three moments of time—the not-yet, the now, and the no-longer—
are expressions of the appeal which man faces at all times. Only in this
area can being be determined—and with it also our behavior towards it.
Insight into the situation occurs in view of the demand which is always
different in the here and now: "Que autem maiora bona et que minora
sunt difficile est pronuntiare, presertim quod *mutantur tempora, loca, per-
sona* et ceteris huiusmodi."[71]

This stresses the importance of the individual case, which traditional
metaphysics, in its desire for the universal, neglects or even regards as
non-essential: "Therefore it is better to determine the single action and
the single thing. I cannot be moderate and immoderate at the same time;
it is more correct to say that I can act rightly or wrongly a thousand times
in the same hour—in the same manner as the same word can be lauded
or vituperated."[72]

Valla's critique of the Aristotelian rational definition of being, which of
all things takes the definition of "fortitudo" as its example, is not accidental: "fortitudo" is a basic attitude and, therefore, exemplary for an exami-
nation of the traditional "ratio vivendi." At the end of his argument Valla
writes: "It is sufficient to have shown the way which one has to go or, as
the saying goes, to have put the finger on the source."[73]

5

Rhetoric as Philosophy

The rational definition of virtue ignores time and place as the "now"
and "here" in which man must respond to the appeal which he always
faces. From this we can draw an essential conclusion: it is not rational
thinking and speaking which prove to be the original philosophical form
but thinking and speaking which occur in view of the situation. The interpretations of being, of the "res," are possible only from the sphere of
the answer responding to the address, and this address becomes known
through enunciating the signification of the words "here" and "now," i.e.,

through rhetoric. The thesis that philosophy therefore must merge with rhetoric is maintained programmatically by Valla: "In fact, philosophy is under the command of rhetoric like a soldier or a tribune; rhetoric rules and, as a great tragedian says, is queen."[74] Valla stresses that such an understanding was the result of his education. "My procedure became possible and permissible because I am free, for I was not introduced to philosophy but to rhetoric and poetry, which are far more important."[75]

Because Cicero, unlike Quintilian, has not sufficiently recognized the identity of philosophy and rhetoric, and has had the audacity to philosophize as philosopher and not as orator, Valla criticizes Cicero and values Quintilian much more highly:

> Cicero has permitted himself to speak freely in philosophy without aligning himself to a sect. In spite of that I would have liked him to use these arguments not as philosopher, but as an orator [mallem ut non tamquam philosophum se illa tractare predicasset, sed tamquam oratorem], and that he should have taken the liberty to elicit from the philosophers all those means of rhetoric which he was able to find among them [. . . ut quicquid oratoris supellectilis apud illos invenisset . . . id omne ab illis fortiter repoposcisset] . . . and I would have wished that he had drawn his sword against these tricksters of philosophy, the sword which he has received from rhetoric to punish them like criminals.[76]

Valla identifies philosophy with rhetoric, quite conscious of the preeminence of the problem of the word above the problem of being.

For this reason, we discover the definition of the "res" through the word in response to the time and the place in which the address speaks. The individual case is of central importance; the individual case is not—as maintained by the Platonists—the accidental, the futile, and unimportant, but quite to the contrary: it is the expression of the situation, of the concrete in the compass of which man always finds himself and in which he answers the demands put to him. It is therefore important to recognize the ever new and varying historical disclosure of Being through the experience of the demands of the word: this is the main problem of philosophy.

From this follows the relationship between philosophy and rhetoric. Valla points out that in the classical tradition rhetoric comprises the realm of the "copia verborum," i.e., the richness of language, the "euporia."[77] He maintains explicitly that the rhetorical ability makes clear the "res" in the context of the "here" and "now" by placing it before our eyes.[78] Rhetorical thinking and speaking—which discover the meaning of beings in the "context" of the historical situation—now come into the foreground. But to begin only with the impassioned commitment of an individual writer—in this case, Valla—in order to define the essence of his rhetorical word, would merely and erroneously psychologize Valla's rhetoric.

6
The Un-attained "Res Religiosa"

We are faced with a fundamental question: what does Valla take to be the human "ratio vivendi" if its interpretation as "honestas" by traditional metaphysics is demonstrably futile? Is it the Epicurean "voluptas?" This can hardly be Valla's intention, for he always makes an effort to construct a "nova ratio" for Christian thought on the debris of a philosophical tradition. In the foreword to the third book he announces his task: he will hold a "de rebus divinis rebus orationem"[79] (for his goal he takes a "divinorum scientiam"[80]), and he proposes a discussion of the "amor divinorum."[81] He wishes to treat the topic with "metus," with "verecundia," and "timor," that is, through rhetorical language. As the starting point of his discussion he will take the love of the divine and the holy: "Nobody can awaken love for the divine if he remains cold for it himself."[82] The divine? But which kind of the divine? It is the same problem which has already arisen in the first part of *De Voluptate:* is nature the appeal in which the "Being-there" stands and for whose response the "voluptas" is the indicating sign? Could nature be the divine? "Idem est enim natura quod Deus aut fere idem?"[83] Suddenly, and without transition, Valla presents—in lieu of the four cardinal virtues—three *theological* virtues as the "ratio vivendi," basing himself on quotations from St. Paul: "fides," "spes," and "amor" (*caritas*). "Paulus cum magno ore proclamat: 'Omne autem quod non est *ex fide* peccatum est'[84] et alibi: 'Iustus *ex fide* vivit,'[85] et iterum: 'Sine fide impossibile est placere Deo.' "[86] After faith, Valla mentions hope and love: "Post fidem et spem tertius est locus *caritatis*, magistre omnium virtutum, *id est amoris* in Deum et proximum."[87] Elsewhere we read: "Amatio ipsa delectatio est, sive voluptas, sive beatitudo sive felicitas sive caritas, qui est finis ultimus et propter quem fiunt cetera."[88]

Valla identifies pleasure (Lust) and the interpretation of this word with the "voluptas" which arises from the theological virtues. "Who would hesitate to find for this felicity [arising from the realization of the theological virtues] a better name than pleasure? I find that in *Genesis* it is spoken of as the 'Paradise of pleasure' where we also read of 'divine pleasure.' And in *Psalms* we read: 'You will drink from the streams of pleasure,' although in Greek the expression has more the meaning of 'enjoyment.' "[89] According to Valla one can therefore maintain that the Divine – as in Psalms 35.9, 10 – is the source of "voluptas" [apud te est fons vitae] and that we see being only through His light, through His transforming fire [et in lumine tuo videbimus lumen].

From this Valla draws some serious consequences, and in doing so he places himself completely within the framework of the Christian tradition: "Nam ea (voluptas) duplex est: altera nunc in terris, altera postea in celis,"[90] and by referring to St. Matthew and St. Luke, Valla maintains that we should "(renunciare) terrenis rebus propter Deum."[91]

Most interpreters see in the preceding theses, in this return to Platonism, a sudden, purely dogmatic turn of our author. But we should now analyse how the "new" thinking to which Valla lays claim is formed. The basis for his philosophy is not, as we saw, the rational thought of demonstration. If being receives its meaning as the response to the appeal, then all existential behavior is based on the *faith* in the unfathomable address. This response to the address occurs in rhetorical, rather than rational, language. Language which realizes itself within the framework of a non-derivative primal instance is at the same time and always the expression of an act of faith, and of a hope without which faith itself would be meaningless. Hope implies per se a letting-be – in the sphere of the individual situation – of an ever newly self-manifesting being. Such recognition therefore demands the affirmation of openness and love.

In our interpretation it becomes clear why Valla replaces the cardinal virtues of classical metaphysics with the three theological virtues, and takes the original pleasure (*voluptas*) to be the "indicating" sign. However, our interpretation excludes the legitimation of transcendence as a "res religiosa" and of the three theological virtues, and – for this very reason – this interpretation questions the validity of Valla's attempt to initiate a new Christian thinking.

The theological virtues indicate only the originality and non-derivability of the appeal in which "being-there" stands *in its historicity*. The contention of a "divina res" (on the basis of which the definition of "voluptas" is thought "paradisical" or "supraterrestial") is not admissible. The "poma et arbor voluptatis," the richness of a transcendent location [ubertas domus tuae], which are derived from the source of pleasure [ex torrente voluptatis] are clearly only words with no corresponding transcendent "res." Faith, hope and love have meaning only in the framework of the "happening" of being, in the process of the self-disclosure of beings, not in any way in the transcending of this horizon.

We can use against Valla the same argument which he attributes to the Epicureans in their critique of the Platonizing "contemplatio." In the second book of *De voluptate* (particularly in connection with the Epicurean critique of "honestas") he states the following: Traditional philosophy holds that man is elevated to a higher divine reality through "honestas": "prestantior atque divinior est illa facies quam ut sub aspectum veniat nostrisque oculis subiiciatur."[92] This tradition thus concludes that "honestas" is the precondition for the "vita contemplativa"—i.e., for a "theoretical" life as the highest level of philosophy: "suam esse vitam contemplativam, suam mentis securitatem. Hec bona solius esse honestatis *et quidem sibi cum diis immortabilibus communia.*"[93]

Aristotle maintains explicitly that the highest activity attainable to man is the intellectual vision;[94] therefore he asserts that the "contemplatio mentis" must be juxtaposed with the "contemplatio oculis."[95] But since the realization of the virtues can be understood anyway only as a response to the demands which man experiences in varying situations, there is no further reason to talk of a "vita contemplativa," of a theoretical "vision" the object of which is an *unhistorical* reality: "Quid enim fere versamus in mente non quasi corporeum, hoc est secundum ea que vidimus, audivimus, aliquo sensu percepimus? Unde contemplatio nata est."[96]

History is the realization of the toilsome disclosure of beings facing the appeal which manifests itself in varying situations. Turning to Aristotle, the Epicurean says: "Nec intelligit [Aristoteles] contemplari nihil aliud quam progressionem esse discendi, quam eandem tum commentationem tum excogitationem dicimus, *quod hominum est et non deorum.*"[97] From this arises the critical question that Valla puts to Aristotle: what kind of lives do the gods live? ". . . non se invicem dii conspiciunt? Non audiunt? Non alloquuntur? Nihil communicant? Nullum amoris mutui et officii indicium exhibent?"[98] The whole argument is important not so much for its criticism of the Aristotelian understanding of the gods, but primarily because the thesis that religious life should take place outside and beyond history is completely emptied of any meaning. Here is that biting and ironic sentence which implicitly attacks Christian philosophy insofar as it bases itself on Aristotle: "It is just as ludicrous to talk of a life of the gods whom we do not know as if we were guessing the life of animals which we do not know."[99]

This argument of the Epicureans, which Valla quotes against Platonic and Aristotelian thought, also has validity as an argument against Valla's own attempt to construct a renewed Christian philosophical thinking on the basis of the problem of "voluptas." The critique of "contemplatio" as the essence of the life of the gods, which Valla puts into the mouths of the opponents of Platonist and Aristotelian philosophy, turns de facto also against his own "new" Christian philosophy. The treatise *De voluptate* concludes with a metaphoric description of paradise as the place of pleasure. Here, too, we have to decide whether this turn in his thought—which is essential for Valla—is philosophically justified, keeping in mind our preceding discussion. After having maintained the preeminence of rhetorical speech, which uses metaphors, over rational speech, which uses concepts, Valla holds that he is justified in proposing a metaphoric description of paradise. However, transference, μεταφέρειν, the employment of an analogy—this is inadmissible for his purpose: maintaining a "res religiosa" on the basis of man's experiences in history as he responds to demands made upon him. A metaphor is possible only if there is a similarity: but between a historical life, with its elements of faith, hope and love, and a suprahistorical reality there can be no "similitudo." In celestial suprahistorical reality the existence of time cannot be assumed, nor can any becoming, or constantly renewed striving, or disclosing; neither has hope, nor faith, nor an anti-dogmatic attitude (*caritas*=openness) any meaning.

It is possible to use the same argument against Valla which he used in the debate between the Stoics and the Epicureans in the second book of *De voluptate*. We find it in an interpretation of the myth of the ring of Gyges. The Stoics and Platonists use this fable to demonstrate to the Epicureans that one must admit that evil remains evil, even if nobody discovers it as such: the good and the evil have their reality *outside* history. The fable reads as follows: a poor shepherd finds a magic ring, becomes king and, after a number of crimes, marries the wife of the king whom he had killed before. All this is possible through the power of the ring. When the ring is turned, the owner of this magic object becomes invisible, and his actions remain hidden from humans and gods alike. Valla uses verbatim Cicero's narrative,[100] which originates from Plato.[101]

The attempt to bring "voluptas" into a relationship with an act of faith, hope, and love *outside of history* (through a metaphor which is supposed to describe the extra-historical place of the "voluptas") turns out to be a "fable"; it is not a real metaphor which "puts something in front of our eyes" through transference. For the ring of Gyges does not exist, and the "similitudo," the precondition of an analogy, is missing. Therefore Valla can affirm: "Because you [the Platonists] are not able to take an example from history, you escape into a fable."[102]

The fact that Valla did not succeed in constructing a new Christian thinking through a critique of Stoicism and Platonism demonstrates once more the difficulties in which Christian thinking finds itself during the period of Humanism. The problem—of the determination of the essence and structure of the original appeal in which the "being-there" stands—thrusts itself ever more urgently into the foreground.

CHAPTER FIVE

History Without Myth

Desiderius Erasmus (1469–1536)
Leon Battista Alberti (1404–1472)
Leonardo da Vinci (1452–1519)

1

Allegorical Language:
The Problem of "Moria"

FOR TRADITIONAL METAPHYSICS THE PROBLEM OF POETRY HAS A DIS-
turbing character. When we drew attention to the controversy between
Mussato and Giovannino of Mantua and to the defense of poetry by Petrarch,
we were able to show the difficulties which result from a scholastic interpretation of poetry. Aristotle asserts that noetic activity is possible only on
the basis of existing "phantasms": "Tὸ νοητικόν ἐν τοῖς φαντάσμασι νοεῖ."[1]
A few lines earlier he maintains that the psyche achieves no insights without
phantasms.[2] Aristotle derives the noun "phantasia" (φαίνεσθαι = appear,
manifest itself) from light, fire. The imaginative faculty is subjected to the
rational process of thought insofar as its images present an εἰκασία, a similarity with that which the senses proffer as material for rational elaboration.
On the other hand, it cannot be denied that in cases where poetic activity
uses images independently of rational control, these appear as unreal, as
purely fantastic, as "untrue" to the scholastic philosopher. But in light of
this, how can poetry be justified? Poetic, metaphorical language can then
only be seen either as a "veiling" of the true, or as a "game," an "escape,"
a "diversion" compared with the demands of reason.

Our problem is the following: do the Humanists, in employing metaphorical thought and speech, have the intention – as traditional thought would

have it—of revealing rational truth beneath the "veil" of images, beneath metaphors—and, if so, why? Or do the Humanists turn back to metaphorical thought and speech in order to acknowledge that it has a specific theoretical function?

For the Humanists—beginning with Dante and down to Mussato, Bruni, Salutati in *De Laboribus Herculis*, Pontano, Guarino und Valla—the poetic, rhetorical word has its own acknowledged function, and even preeminence over rational thought and language. It is impossible to speak "rationally" about the primal, the non-deducible, the pre-eminent—and, as such, the unfathomable. The non-deducible can have its claim adequately responded to only in metaphors—in the realm of the "here" and "now" and through the word of "indication" rather than "proof," through mythical rather than rational language. Only in this way can it be uncovered, unveiled. Only in this form of expression can it manifest its εἰχασία and therewith its response to the primal, which cannot be grasped in a purely rational manner.

Every historical epoch proceeds from mythical (and, in consequence, "evangelical") proclamations, which at various times provide the basis for the different social, political, moral institutions and assertions. This reversal of traditional thinking can only come about within the framework of an epistemology that proceeds from the problem of the word and its "ingenious" function.

In this context our attention is drawn to a fundamental problem. What do the Humanists mean when they speak of poetry as a "second theology," as a "second philosophy"; or, rather, what interpretation do they place upon the existential claim, which man can meet only through metaphorical language? In order to answer this question we must turn to a text by Erasmus of Rotterdam, which gives an answer at once dramatic, ironic, and metaphorical.

Erasmus wrote *Moriae Encomium* (*The Praise of Folly*) during his return journey north from Italy—from the Rome of the Popes. It is an allegorical oration consisting of a string of metaphors, by no means a philosophical treatise in the traditional sense. The work arose—according to Erasmus—from the "pleasure derived from an ingenious game"; more precisely, from delight in the pun on the word "moria" and the name of his friend Thomas More, to whom the work is dedicated [admonuit me Mori cognomen tibi gentile, quod tam ad Moriae vocabulum accedit].[3]

In order to comprehend the full impact of this work, and interpret it objectively, we must begin by clarifying the term "moria." The various translations of the Greek expression μωρία already point to its ambiguity. In the Latin formulation, which was chosen by Erasmus himself, the term is "stultitia"; the English translation of the Greek title is *The Praise of Folly*, the German *Lob der Torheit*, the Italian *Elogio della pazzia* ("Praise of Mania.") Μωρός means "dull," "stupid," and refers to a physical and mental deficiency. With reference to man this expression is generally used psychologically to denote a general inferiority in thought and behavior.[4] As a result of "moria," man succumbs to a prevailing power, which confuses his intelligence and leads him to manic actions.[5]

In the Septuagint—in the *Book of Proverbs* and in the *Book of Wisdom*—the word "μορός" refers to one who lacks φρόνησις, who is consequently not σώφρων, not rational, and therefore achieves neither a knowledge of God nor any rational insight. It is he who, having eyes, sees not, and having ears, hears not.[6] As used by Paul (in the New Testament) the terms μωρία and "stultitia" undergo a fundamental transformation.[7] For Paul, worldly wisdom is a "stultitia" in the face of God; here the term retains its original negative meaning. Christian faith, however, is derided as foolishness by the philosophers of Athens, the men who have worldly wisdom. Therefore Paul polemically identifies "moria" with the true original knowledge, because in the estimation of the world the Christians with their faith were considered to be "stulti." What the Greek men of learning reject as "stultitia" is elevated by Paul to be the sign of "true knowledge"; the Christian warning is: he who wishes to be "wise" will appear "foolish" in the eyes of his fellow men. This meaning of "stultus" is still found in Luther. In his preface to the translation of the Old Testament he warns the reader "that he is not to take offense at the simple language and story, which he will often encounter, but rather doubt not, however mean they may appear to be, that these be the pure word, work, judgment, and history, of the high divine majesty, power, and wisdom. For this is the book which makes fools of the wise and clever and is open only to the lowly and foolish, as Christ says."[8]

So what is *Moriae Encomium* all about? Is it a "praise of folly," that is, "human" behavior? Does the treatise confine itself merely to this—in other words, is it an "ironical" anthropology—or is it something far more fundamental, a treatise about Being and its self-disclosure?

To begin with, it must be pointed out that "moria" does *not* refer *only* to the human sphere: it is not concerned with a human problem. Erasmus explicitly gives "Moria" the status of a deity, who can claim to reveal "being in its totality." He says: "She is a power, active in the entire world and will not let herself be reduced to a formula, and a deity in whose worship all beings unite must not be dismembered " [. . . cuius numen tam late pateat . . . in cuius cultum omne rerum genus ita consentiat].[9]

Under the sign of "Moria" being discloses itself in its diverse forms of life. Thus Erasmus speaks of the "brutorum ingenium stultitiamque,"[10] pointing out that the beasts are happy because they submit to the "plan" of life devised by "Moria" without reflection. Genius (*ingenium*) – in its original meaning as we encountered it earlier among the Latin scholars – would hardly have been mentioned fortuitously by Erasmus in connection with "stultitia." "Moria" does not stand simply for a way of being human, for a human condition, namely, folly. It is also the epitome of the appealing power through which all being manifests itself in its semantic significance; it is the pervasive power, which cannot be explained or derived: the unfathomable.

According to Erasmus, "Moria" was born on the Isle of the Blessed, "where no one sows and no one plows, where everything sprouts of itself" [in ipsis insulis fortunatis, ubi ἄσπαρτα καὶ ἀνήροτα omnia proveniunt. In quibus neque labor neque senium, neque morbus est ullus].[11] Thus "Moria" is here equated with φύσις as the essence of the eternal φυεῖν, growing, sprouting. In the realm of "physis" every death is always also a birth. Erasmus underscores this idea by emphasizing that here neither toil nor old age nor illness are known.

With polemic intention Erasmus lets "Stultitia" make the claim that she – as the original ruling power – needs neither temple nor ritual, in fundamental contrast to all ancient and contemporary religions. In this connection, she says: "What I call religious homage is that I be loved in the heart, acknowledged in conduct, embodied in way of life" [Ego me tum religiosissime coli puto, cum passim ut faciunt omnes animo complectuntur, moribus exprimunt, vita repraesentant].[12] The acknowledgment of "Stultitia" is rooted in the heart of man, and she says (polemically aiming at religious institutions): "Why should I lay claim to a little cloud of incense or bruised grain . . . when the entire earth worships me in just the manner that the theologians recommend most?" [Praeterea cur templum desiderem, cum orbis hic universus templum mihi sit, ni fallor, pulcherrimum?][13]

2

The Mask

The *Encomium* rests on the question of what it is that manifests itself to man as a result of the claims of "Moria." What is at issue is the setting up of the stage on which world history takes place. The works and institutions of history reveal themselves only in the realm of "Moria"—not in the realm of rational thought.

The great charm and affirmation of life—a token of youth, which, in its unencumbered "mania," is capable of achieving the apparently impossible—arises from a deficiency in "ratio." It is one of the achievements of "Moria" if, for instance, old age does not show itself to man in all its cruelty and ugliness. All antiquity—so Erasmus elaborates—laments the process of aging, with its infirmity, ugliness and ill health. So Homer (*Odyssey* 8.102), so Vergil (*Aeneid* 9.388), so Seneca (*Oedipus* 594). Only by succumbing to the power of "Moria" does man save himself from a disgust with life: "Non sentit vitae taedium."[14] "Moria," which conceals from man the consciousness of imminent death, helps him to glide out of life imperceptibly: "Quoque magis accedunt ad senectam, hoc propius ad pueritiae similitudinem redeunt, donec puerorum ritu citra vitae taedium, citra mortis sensum emigrant e vita."[15]

And what is the desire of the scholar other than a special manner of remaining under the influence of a "mania?" Seriousness and constant strenuous thought sap the scholar of his vital spirit; only on the basis of the mania that governs them do scholars become capable of believing that they can create a masterpiece if they weave a Greek word "like a colored thread" into a Latin text. Here the polemical attitude of Erasmus towards traditional philosophy and its proponents finds expression: "You can see for yourselves: these melancholic people, who sell themselves to philosophy or to earnest serious work, are usually senile old men before they have ever been properly young . . . because their seriousness and their eternal strenuous thinking robs them of all their liveliness, all their sap."[16]

How does the world of man come to be? Erasmus attributes to "Moria" a metaphoric and metamorphic power: it is through her that man achieves his essential nature: "Ego vero hominem eundem optimae ac felicissimae vitae parti restituo."[17] Erasmus emphasizes that the transforming power of "Moria" is radically different from the metamorphosis, which we encounter in the ancients, for the changes the ancients describe destroy man as such: Daphne becomes a tree, Ciris a bird, Cadmus a snake;[18] whereas the transforming power of metaphor, which derives from "Moria," lets man be what he is, and more, allows him to manifest himself through it.

But how does this transformation occur, which permits a creature to call himself a man (entitles him to the pretension of being human), and which allows him to be at the same time a creature and something different —namely, a man? Through the mask which "Moria" puts on him. Through it men make their appearance as actors; in the function of the role of the moment they are given the necessary masks. In and through the mask "Moria" at once reveals and conceals herself; she rules the world and lets her diverse "histories" appear.

At this point our real problem emerges. When Erasmus says it is "Moria" who provides man with his masks, does this mean that these masks— which are closely connected with the political, social, legal, religious institutions of the times—are the expression of something divine, in the Platonic or Christian sense? For example, traditionally reason (*ratio*) is differentiated from the instinctive passions (*affectio*). Proceeding from this dualism the Stoic brands passion as foolishness [perturbationes omnes ceu morbos a sapiente semovent];[19] in other words, man dons the mask of the Stoic ethic. But it is merely a mask behind which no new reality is concealed. It is—as Erasmus emphasizes—a false and "empty" one. For if wisdom consisted solely in the activity of reason, then even Jupiter would recognize such a life to be sad and dismal, "tristis ac tetrica";[20] a "marble, lifeless, false image of man."[21]

Furthermore: "The human race is propagated neither through the spear of Pallas, nor through Zeus, the collector of clouds, but by sensual pleasure alone. Therefore if Zeus begets a child he will have to leave at home at the last moment his divine mask, likewise his three-pronged thunderbolt, and his Titan's mien" [fulmen illud trisulcum ponat oportet et vultum illum Titanicum, quo, cum lubet, Deos omneis territat, planeque histrionum more aliena sumenda misero persona].[22] Likewise, the Stoic—who condemns all things sensual as vain and despicable—will retain but his beard as his insignia of wisdom. Incidentally, Erasmus remarks, "the billygoat too has a beard" [barba, insigne sapientiae, etiam si cum hircis commune].[23] There is no doubt that he will have to lower his haughty brows, smooth his lined forehead and drop his adamant principles [abiicienda

dogmata illa adamantina].²⁴ "For what part of man"—Erasmus asks—
"serves procreation? Neither the head, nor the face nor the breast, nor
the hand or the ear, but something so ludicrous, so foolish, that it can't
be mentioned without laughter" [pars adeo stulta adeoque ridicula, vt nec
nominari citra risum possit].²⁵

3

The Demythicization of History:
"Moria" as Tragic Illusion:
The Antiplatonism of Erasmus

In order to realize his own existence man must respond to the appeal
of "Moria." Is there an element of the divine manifested in the undeduced
and unfathomable nature of "Moria" [cuius numen tam late pateat]?²⁶
Only the answer to this question can lead to an understanding of the nature of the appeal. Erasmus replies with scathing answers, which we cite
here in detail.

1. The various fables enacted by man on the stage of the world are in
truth a mere comedy, and a ludicrous one at that, since the performers
acting on the stage believe that they are "selves" capable of thinking and
speaking independently; they do not notice that they stand under the spell
of "Moria," who prescribes the masks they should wear and the corresponding roles. People do not realize that everything that comes to pass in this
way is a hollow masquerade. At the decisive moment, when the masks—
of the statesman, of natural pride, of the custodian of institutions, and,
last but not least, of the representatives of religions—fall away,²⁷ it becomes evident that they conceal only "mania," self-assertiveness, ambition, the lust for power, sensuality. The masks bring about a metamorphosis,
but this "transfer" is only external; the mask hides nothing "new" behind it.
  In this context Erasmus draws attention to a tragically grotesque image:
he compares the "addiction" of the "spectators of the world-plays"—he
means the "theorists" of the human "spectacle"—with the tragic delusion
of the man from Argos, who sat alone in an empty theatre for days at a

time, weeping, laughing, enjoying, in the manic delusion that something was happening there, that wonderful dramas were being enacted, whereas in fact the stage was empty [Argivus ille, qui hactenus insaniebat, ut totos dies solus desideret in theatro ridens, plaudens, gaudens, quod crederet illic miras agi tragoedias, cum nihil omnino ageretur].[28]

2. If the theorist – the spectator – recognizes what has come into the "clearing"on stage as no more than a ludicrous comedy, because all institutions, the ideals of scholarship, the veneration of art, even war and peace, merely mask primeval drives, then human history must be regarded as the ultimate tragedy. If, however, in accordance with what has been said earlier, the manifestations of "Moria" disclose the unity of comedy and tragedy, then the simultaneity of tragedy and comedy, of tears and laughter – that is, contradiction – is the essence of history.

3. If the above-mentioned insight (θεωρία) contained the essence of wisdom, then it could be assumed that the most urgent task for the theorist (the "spectator" of the world theatre, the philosopher) would be the unmasking of the various actors. This, however, would prove to be pure "madness," for the moment the mask of the actor is torn off, the possibility of performing the play is destroyed. "If someone were to tear the mask from the face of the actor on stage to reveal to the spectator the true, natural faces he would turn the whole play upside down . . . Everything would gain a new face . . . He, who until then had been a god, would appear as a poor devil . . . If the illusion is destroyed, then the play is spoilt" [Verum eum errorum tollere est fabulam omnem perturbare . . . Adumbrata quidem omnia, sed haec fabula non aliter agitur].[29] The worst is, therefore, not so much the delusion in which we live, but – as the knowing would have us do – no longer submitting to the illusions, for by doing that we would destroy life itself: "Sed falli, inquiunt, miserum est. *Imo non falli, miserrimum.*"[30] Knowledge as the highest form and essence of human endeavor is equal to "mania": the irrationality of rationality, the senselessness of the θεωρεῖν.

Thus "moria" undergoes a radical change in the course of the text, and this in definite contrast to Paul's Christian interpretation. It acquires the meaning of "mania," of "delusion," in which and through which man reveals himself, a meaning of "mania" in the Middle High German sense of the word "wân": hope, expectation. "Wân" includes other meanings as well: of striving for, of winning, becoming accustomed to, delight, and wish. This "magic," this transforming claim and appeal, proves in the further development of the text to be "madness" (folly, *pazzia*) and, finally, illusion (*dementia, stultitia*).

Erasmus is aware of the need to point out the radical difference between his interpretation of illusion and the Platonic interpretation of "mania." He mentions the three forms of illusion about which Plato writes: that of the poet, that of the prophet, and that of the lover;[31] he refers to *Phaedrus* (244a). According to the Platonic interpretation, the "divine" manifests itself in all three. But not only through these three forms of "mania" may we overcome the human comedy and return to the realm of truth that transcends the relative, the world of shadows. To reveal this higher reality – or, rather, to bring about this transcendence – is also the business of the philosopher as metaphysician. In the parable of the cave Plato makes a radical distinction between the negative aspect of the world of shadows, which exists *within* the cave, and the reality, which exists *behind* and *above* the shadow-world, that is, outside of it or, more precisely, "above" it.

Erasmus is fully aware of the difference between his nihilistic conception of history and Plato's conception: "Est alterum huic longe dissimile, quod videlicet a me proficiscitur."[32] The basically anti-Platonic trend of the *Encomium* shows up in Erasmus' polemic rejection of the distinction between those who see (supernatural, unhistorical) reality as such, and those who only live, think, and act in the realm of shadows, or, better, in the history of the human comedy.

Erasmus poses the following question: Why should those who live in the world of shadows, and think and act according to their illusion, flee the cave? There is no difference between those who live in the cave and enjoy the magic of the shadow-images and their variety (and consequently strive for nothing else), and the wise man who has left the cave to see reality as such. [Num quid interesse censetis inter eos, qui in specu illo Platonico variarum rerum umbras ac simulacra demirantur, modo nihil desiderent neque minus sibi placeant, et sapientem illum, qui specum egressus veras res adspicit?][33]

The blissfulness which characterizes the human comedy is not attributed to the divine, that is, to the "new" that resides "over" and "above" human history (and therefore transcends it): it may be found only by abandoning yourself totally to the appeal of "moria," which is experienced in history: ". . . . iucundus quidam mentis error simul et anxiis illis curis animum liberat."[34]

One could ask oneself how it was possible for Erasmus to demythicize "moria"—in which St. Paul saw the essence of the religious—and to do so in that particular period. Martin Dorp's accusation that the *Encomium* made fun of eternal life is fully justified. Erasumus also had to defend himself against the criticisms of Alberto Pio da Carpi.[36] But in the *Encomium* our author forestalls criticism by pointing out that it is not possible to express profound thoughts in other than rhetorical form, since irony and metaphor are the only modes suited to expressing thought without alienating readers or listeners. A gift of this nature is peculiar to those who stand in the power of "Moria": a confession that could cost the wise man his life becomes a source of merriment if spoken by a "madman" [a morione profectum, incredibilem voluptatem pariat].[37]

That is a tragic verdict passed on human historicity, which forces us to draw the same conclusions as in the case of Valla. If the appeal of "Moria," which man must respond to as the occasion demands, cannot be rationally accounted for, then it is she who distributes the different parts in the drama of world history and provides men with their various masks. If, however, the structure of "Moria" is unfathomable because it cannot be rationally clarified, then the revelation of the essence of being through "Moria" implies an act of faith (*fides*). Such an unveiling of the meaning of being has as its prerequisite hope (*spes*), for in the original appeal, in which man himself appears, he must remain "open" for every new form of self-manifesting. The denial of hope would mean that faith, in whose realm man finds self-realization, would become untenable. Finally, this faith—which rises from "moria"—forces man to reject every form of dogmatism, which prevents the new from making itself known. Accordingly, the appeal of "Moria" does not demand only the existential attitudes of faith and hope, but likewise that of "caritas," that is, the three attitudes which tradition has laid down as the theological "virtues." If in the *Moriae Encomium* the theological virtues result from the structure of "Moria," they do not, however, profess the "transcendent" but—in the course of their demythicizing—show themselves to be a "Christian illusion."

The interpretation which we have given of the *Encomium* may appear absurd, since Erasmus was the very Humanist who put his greatest efforts into reintroducing the authors of the Greek and Latin tradition into the realm of the Christian tradition. Consequently, we must ask ourselves these questions: Does the reversion to allegorical, metaphorical discourse on the part of the Humanists result from a consciousness of the limitations of rational thought, of the "appropriate" expression which is logically defined? Does metaphorical discourse therefore have a specific philosophical mission?

If the Humanist identifies the nature of the word with the "tropus," that is, with its transferable character, is then the problem of a logical "truth" — which is valid at all times and in all places — replaced by the question of what "reveals" itself in the historical process from time to time? And, finally, does the Humanist offer a new interpretation of "theory" through this reversal? These are problems to which Vico will return, when he counters Cartesian thought; problems, moreover, which the Platonizing and Aristotelizing philosophy of the Renaissance will in part leave behind.

4

The "Momus" of Leon Battista Alberti

The questions we have raised form the central focus of Alberti's *Momus*, a metaphorical speculative critique of traditional thought. Let us keep the following dates in mind: *Momus* — many of its theses are also found in Alberti's *Intercoenales* — was written between 1443 and 1450, but was only posthumously published, twice in Rome in 1520, and was translated into Spanish in the following years and into German in the eighteenth century. Erasmus wrote his *Encomium* in 1509, Machiavelli his *Prince* around 1517, and Luther published his theses in 1517: these are the years in which traditions are radically re-examined.

Lucian of Samosate provides Alberti's literary model. The title of his work refers to the main protagonist of his metaphorical debate: Momus. Mythological sources point to Momus as the embodiment of the critical mind. According to Hesiod (*Theogony* 214), Momus belongs to the second generation of the children of Nyx: as the son of sleep and night he is the god of mischievous pranks; it is his business to expose and criticize the errors of men and of gods. In Lucian, Momus ridicules Neptune, Vulcan and Minerva: he advises Zeus to reduce the numbers of men by begetting a mortal being (Helen), who will create the antagonism between Europe and Asia. This explains the origin of the Trojan war.

Alberti introduces the main protagonist of his work as the embodiment of the constantly critical mind; with this attitude Momus reveals himself also as the tragic court jester. The first question we must raise: What is the function of the metaphorical mode of Alberti's text? In accordance with its own declaration, the work is written in this manner to treat serious themes in a humorous, joking manner. In this way the reader experiences pleasure: ". . . instituat dictorum gravitate rerumque dignitate varia et eleganti, idemque una risu illectet, jocis delectet, voluptate detineat."[38] The intention is that the meaning and function of philosophical activity will be understood more profoundly by means of the metaphor [versari me in quodam philosophandi genere minime aspernando].[39] Through allegory — as we shall see — the nature of man (that which makes him resemble the gods) is identified with his metamorphic, metaphorical ability.

In *Momus* man's divine ability is defined as a "sacred fire," as an eternal flame [perpetua lucescat flammis], which turns everything that it touches into something immortal: "immortales, incorruptibilesque reddat." From this man's talents derive: ". . . solis in villis mapparum, quas dea Virtus contexuit, sacer ipse ignis vigeat." It is the very same fire which also shines from the brow of the gods [sacro ex foco hausta flammula ad summum frontis verticem quibusque deorum illucet]; its power resides in the transformation of things [. . . in quas velint rerum formas sese queant ex arbitrio vertere]."[40]

So, not reason (*ratio*), but the power to transform unites men and gods: Prometheus robbed the gods of a spark of this fire and gave it to man [Hoc ex foco cum Prometheus radium subripuisset]. Through this man attains the divine, rising to the level of the immortal, the eternal.[41] The importance of this thesis can be comprehended if we look at Momus' revolutionary judgment of Jupiter. The goddess of deceit causes Momus to express his opinion about the ruler of Olympus. The answer is categorical: the god of eternal, unhistorical reality must be a madman; in order to save himself the effort, he has handed over the management of the divine fire to Fate: "Fato deo . . . summamque ignium potestatem legavit."[42] But it should be pointed out that the goddess Verina (a goddess who does not exist in the classical Olympus and who is called "temporis enim dei filiam" by Alberti)[43] betrays Momus to the gods.

This leads to the following revolutionary deduction: If the management of the divine fire is no longer in the hands of Zeus, but is left to Fate, then the eternal order of things, which had till now been guaranteed by

the ruler, no longer exists: Jupiter, as the one and only ruler, is replaced
by other gods, and history will break into the realm of the eternal.[44] With
his critical intellect, Momus therefore announces the dissolution of the ruling
and previously unhistorical eternal order: history enters into the realm of
the divine; Momus is in reality the one who calls the divine world into
question, and he thus becomes involved in grotesque adventures and is
trusted by no one. That is also why Momus is exiled from Olympus, from
the previously unhistorical, eternal world. So we have here a double reversal
of traditional thinking: the preeminence of the metaphorical and metamorphic over rational activity, and the eruption of history into the realm of the
eternal; the most diverse gods will rule in the course of history and
metaphorical thought and speech will prove to be the root of historicity.

In his exile on earth Momus undertakes his fight against the gods [Etru-
riam ab deorum cultu . . . abducere][45] and writes irreverent poetry and
heretical treatises. Traditionally the virtues (*virtutes*) and their outward recognition (praise, fame after death, triumphal columns, trophies) represent
the motives of human actions. As a result of the demythologizing of the
gods and the entrance of history into the realm of the divine, questions
arise: are the virtues and the judgments they extol in reality something
divine and should they be recognized as "rationes vivendi?" We find the
same problem that Valla raised. The "idols" too, for whose sake men act
and sacrifice themselves, Alberti demythologizes: fame is unmasked as
a mystification of praise; all victories—from Marathon to those of the Roman battlefields—are evaluated as the result of coincidence and good
luck.[46] Alberti gives expression to this idea in another allegorical story.

Momus' polemics against the gods are so successful that it is decided
on Olympus to send a goddess, who is universally esteemed and honored,
down to earth: it is hoped that thereby the renown and dignity of the gods
can be restored. Virtue (*virtus*) is chosen, along with her four offspring:
Praise (*laus* is feminine in Latin), Tropheus, Triumph and Subsequent Fame
[hos laute ornatos secum dea proficiscens ducit, per quos, sin aliter ne-
queat, deorum veteres hospites, proceres mortalium heroasque . . .
moveat].[47]

The arrival of the goddess Virtue—with her progeny—does not only
arouse high expectations among humans: the ancient Italic gods too hope
that in this way their dignity will be acclaimed once more.[48] But Momus
falls in love with Laus and, through his metamorphic ability (which, as
a god, he retains even in exile), he transforms himself into ivy—a metaphor

for faithfulness and constancy. Laus combs her hair and weaves ivy leaves into it, and is thus raped by Momus: she gives birth to a monster, Fame (*fama*). This name is derived from "fari" (talk): "Abi tu . . . malam in rem, Fama, quandoquidem fari non desinis."[49]

No sooner is it born than this monster flutters around the world, announcing to all that neither Tropheus, nor Triumph, nor Praise nor Subsequent Fame are children of Virtue—as had been generally assumed—but of Chance and Fortune: "Triumphum enim Trophaeumque non Virtute natos, sed Casus Fortunaeque filios, et eorum alterum esse stolidum, alterum dementem adiurabat."[50] Even Subsequent Fame is ridiculed: he is incapable of walking for "his feet are turned backwards."

This demythicizing of the basic motives of human action occurs in a still more radical manner with Alberti's new, anti-traditional interpretation of the myth of Hercules, the very Hercules who is, traditionally, the symbol of man's ingeniousness. According to the ancient legend, Hercules battles against the monsters of the world and thereby achieves his fame. Alberti reverses this myth: Fortuna hears that Virtue has decided to rule the earth once more in the place of Fortuna [Virtuti ob eam rem infensa, quod iam pridem constituendarum rerum apud mortales provinciam affectasset].[51] With the intention of leading man back to the realm of the gods, the sacred fire of Virtue is once more lit upon an altar [Virtutem instituisse in ara apud mortales focum succendere divorum flamma, quo mortalibus in astra pateret via].[52] Virtus assumes the power of Hercules, in order to slay Fortuna (a last desperate attempt to gain recognition for the concept of *virtus*). But by means of a ruse, Fortuna succeeds in abducting Hercules and taking him to the Olympic heaven.[53] So it is not the Herculean deeds that bring fame to Virtue, but the reverse; a monster that came into being through the rape of Praise makes it possible to say of the deeds of Hercules: Through them Hercules is praised to Olympus!

This myth demonstrates to us a renewed denial of rationalistic tradition. Allegory, satire, irony: here we have the focal point of the metaphoric thinking and writing of Alberti. Through the web of his myths and the inner continuity of his ingenious inventions our author gradually reveals a radical and systematic demythicizing of traditional values.

5

The Concept of "Experience" in Leonardo da Vinci (1452–1519)

At this point we must interrupt our discussion of *Momus*. We have pointed out often enough how Platonizing thought begins with universal principles and deduces knowledge of being from them: therefore arriving at an essentially "un-historical" knowledge. According to this approach, ingenious thought means contemplation of the eternal world of ideas: history is then the account of man's attempts to reduce the real to eternal "symbols," or rather, an account of his success or failure, as the case may be.

Through their interpretations of texts the Humanists have, instead, found out that the word cannot be identified with its rational unhistorical designation. In turning back to this philologic experience and to the anti-Platonism of Alberti it becomes clear that the concept of experience (*esperienza*) moves into the foreground. Leonardo da Vinci's discussion of "esperienza" enables us to assess the full significance of this concept in the context of Humanist thought.

The writings of Leonardo seem to originate in a polemic attitude to the Humanist tradition to which we have drawn attention. Leonardo speaks of himself as "a man without a sense of literature" [io essere omo senza lettere][54] and refers to the criticisms levelled against him: "Because I have no literary training, I cannot formulate what I wish to say [. . . per non avere io lettere non potere bene dire quello, che voglio trattare].[55] His polemic against the "lettere" is, in fact, a criticism of every ossified tradition and every form of dogmatism, a criticism based on the clear understanding that every authority has arisen from an original effort (*fatica*), which is what matters. When Leonardo rails against "those who preen themselves with the results of another's efforts and refuse to recognize mine" [quelli che dell' altrui fatiche se medesimi fanno ornati le mie a me medesimo non vogliono concedere],[56] he is referring to the effort of "experience": "My things are derived more from experience than from the words of others" [le mie cose sono più da esser tratte dall' esperienza che d'altrui parola].[57] Leonardo expressly calls himself "the disciple of experience" [Leonardo da Vinci discepolo dell'esperienza]:[58] though of course the disciple of the experience of "nature," not of "texts."

Is there at the same time an identity and a difference between the interpreter of nature – as Leonardo sees him – and the interpreter of texts, and if this is so, where does it lie? To both, every *a priori*, abstract designation of an expression is alien; the meaning of a term can only arise from an investigation of either nature or the texts. The "texts" alone – as evidence of reality forcing itself upon us – differ for the scientist and the philologist. Let us keep in mind Leonardo's thesis: "Men are *discoverers* and *interpreters* between nature and man" [li uomini *inventori* ed *interpreti* tra la natura e gli uomini].[59] The natural scientist – like the philologist – is "interpreter" and "discoverer." Nature and texts both will only communicate in the context of the questions that are posed: natural science (*scienza*) is the philology of nature.

Leonardo defines experience (*esperienza*) in the following manner: "Experience – interpreter between inventive nature and human kind – teaches us: what nature, forced by necessity, creates among mortals cannot be anything that reason, her rudder, did not teach her to bring about" [La sperienza, interprete infra l'artificiosa natura e la umana specie, ne insegna ciò che essa natura in fra mortali adopera, da necessità costretta non altrimenti operar si possa che la ragione, suo timone, operare le insegni].[60] Through experiment, necessity, the law, and the foundations of nature are discovered; through it man is freed of every arbitrariness. "Necessity is theme and discoverer of nature and the eternal check and rule" [La necessità è tema ed inventrice della natura, è freno e regola eternal].[61]

Because experience unveils for us the necessity of nature, it distances us from pure sense impressions, which only transmit the subjective: the "necessities," however, reveal themselves only through experience and never through abstraction. Without the senses any form of experience would be impossible, but since the necessity of the causes only manifests itself through experience, this is distinct from mere mediation of the senses: "The senses are of this earth, reason is always apart from them when it contemplates" [I sensi sono terrestri, la ragione sta fuor di quelli quando contempla].[62] Consequently "things of the mind, in so far as they have not come the way of the senses, are idle" [Le cose mentali che non sono passate per il senso sono vane].[63] The possibility of "interpreting" nature, of "explaining" it and thereby making it "speak out," offers itself only in this manner. Certainty (*certezza*) derives from experience,[64] and, since the questions that are put to nature arise from ever different pressures, Leonardo reveals a totally anti-Platonic thesis: "Truth was but the daughter of time" [La venrità fu sola figliola del tempo].[65]

When Leonardo speaks of the "nature" he investigates it is not something in itself given and determined – as in Lucretius – but a nature receiving
her significance exclusively through the human genius, which reveals her
necessity through the experimental process. Consequently, Leonardo never
defines nature: she remains a mystery that is only revealed, as the occasion would have it, by means of the questions which urge themselves upon
man: "Nature is full of reasons that have never been experienced" [La
natura è piena d'infinite ragioni che non furono mai in esperienza].[66] That
is the reason for Leonardo's criticism of those who assert that "only the
knowledge that begins and ends in the mind is scientific" [. . . essere scien-
tifica quella conoscenza che nasce e finisce nella menta].[67] It is, therefore, impossible to speak of "nature" outside the boundaries of experience.
Platonism of every kind is remote from Leonardo, who will never derive
the meaning of existence from abstract ideas or the respective ontology.

Being reveals itself to him only through his anatomical research and
his artistic representations of natural phenomena. The danger associated
with this anti-traditional and anti-Platonic attitude explains the meaning
of his utterance: "and I would say still more, if I were permitted to declare
the truth completely" [. . . e più oltre direi, se'l dire il vero mi fussi integral-
mente lecito],[68] a confession arising from his contempt of human stu-
pidity.

6

A New Interpretation of Socratic Dialogue and Apollo's Love of the Night

It is only through these introductory comments about Leonardo's concept of "experience" that an understanding of an important passage of Alberti's *Momus* becomes possible: a rejection of the Platonic tradition and
thereby of the traditional interpretation of Socrates. In Alberti's mythical
fable, Jupiter, concerned about a "reform" of the world, comes down to
earth. Mercury and Apollo are given the same mission: namely, to discover whether the philosophers can offer suggestions for a "reform." The
report about the philosophers turns out to be totally negative: they never
agree about anything, each considers the others mad, they usually have

bad characters, and at the smallest provocation they show themselves to be quarrelsome and aggressive [in stultitia congruunt . . . quod quisque probat, alios non probare . . . vix feras tantam in sapientiae professoribus versari insaniam].[69]

The Platonists are ridiculed because they waste their time uselessly searching for Plato in their Academy "by the light of glow-worms, without finding him."[70] The Cynics are concerned only with criticizing and insulting each other [omnibus maledicere et mordere],[71] and their rejection of social life is condemned as a form of madness [ne vero is non furor est, nolle rebus perfrui quae ad cultum, ad victum faciant, quibus caeteri omnes mortales utantur? . . . stultitia est].[72] The empiricist's efforts to find the seat of the passions are also ridiculed.[73] Alberti analyses the various conflicts between the philosophical theories.

And now we reach the central point of his discussion: a conversation between Socrates and a tradesman in the presence of Apollo, which aroused the interest of Jupiter; he demands an exact report of it and, as he stresses, without any interpretation on the part of others [cupiam de eo audire, quae vere sua quidem sint, *non quae aliena fictione Socratis dicantur*].[74] Obviously neither Xenophon nor Plato are recognized as interpreters: in fact, the text of Alberti gives expression to a wholly anti-Platonic interpretation of the Socratic dialogue.

The point in question is a determination of the source of man's creative activity, the nature of his ποίησις. The text follows the model of the Socratic dialogue and comes to the following conclusions: If a cobbler wants to make a pair of shoes [si quid in mentem tibi veniat ut velis optimum calceum conficere], he must first *choose* the best leather [tibi corio esse opus statues optimo . . . ex multis commodius *eligas*]; furthermore, he must execute his choice on the basis of *experience* [quod experiundo videris corium peropportunum . . . propones tibi], for the best leather is chosen for a reason (*ratio*) and not by chance (*casus*), and moreover with the intention of avoiding every mistake [qui vero optimum illud condidit corium, casune an ratione assecutus est, ut illi nullae adessent mendae?]. The "ratio" of the work therefore consists in its *use* (*usus*)—for what purpose the leather is to be used—and in *experience* (*experientia*) [condiendi corii *usu* et *experientia* perceperat].[75]

The transformation (*metamorphose*) of any material therefore does not happen on the basis of the contemplation (θεωρία) of abstract ideas, but of "usus" and "experientia": ". . . ita ille in parando corio similitudinibus utebatur, partes partibus, integrumque integro comparans, quod futurum corium omnibus numeris responderet suo huic, quod menti memoriae- que ascriptum tenebat corium."[76] Human work is understood as a response to demands made on man in the situation he happens to be in, and therewith, at the same time, as the celebration of being in the context of the situation at hand, in which this work appears with ever new mean- ings. Thus the traditional Platonic interpretation of Socrates, who is seen as falling back on the world of the eternal unhistoric ideas for the expla- nation of ποίησις is rejected as a distortion. So Jupiter's wish to receive a report about the Socratic dialogue "without the mediating interpretation of others" becomes comprehensible.

We have said: traditionally, the "true" meaning of an expression was considered the outcome of its rational fixation, which would determine it once and for all. Accordingly, the metaphor (figurative speech which pre- supposes a "similitudo") was rejected by logic as an inaccurate form of expression. Instead, Alberti recognizes that man is always encountering new existential situations and thus falling back on translations, metaphors, to do justice to them. Although metaphorical thought and speech do not belong to the province of logic, Alberti is forced to accord them a philosophi- cal function. On the basis of the problematic here discussed the metaphorical coherence of Alberti becomes intelligible.

The demythicizing of the traditional motives of historical action in the first book of *Momus* implies a renewed clarification of the motives of hu- man activity and, therefore, of the impulses that lead to social communi- ty: hence the necessity to examine in this context the problem of politics posed later in this book. Indeed, after his exile to earth, Momus is once again admitted to the divine Olympus and summoned by the gods to report on the social, political life of humankind: "Demum sic statuo oportere his quibus intra multitudinem atque in negocio vivendum sit."[77] And so Al- berti's work is also given the title *De Principe* (along with *Momus*) and count- ed with the political writings of Humanism.

The judgment Alberti passes upon human society and politics is cynical and radically negative. Men deceive each other; they give each other promises which they do not keep (and are always prepared to execute the reverse); so the world is ruled by deceit and chance, al- though men conceal this insight from the people and strive to achieve glory through idle and bombastic talk.[78] Human life in its profound dishonesty proves to be sadder and more unhappy than that of beasts [. . . eosdem inferiore sorte quam bruta pleraque animantia agere vitam].[79]

Momus reports that within the confines of human politics the art of flattery, and the ability to hide your own opinions and intentions play the most important role: it is possible to rule only by means of deceit, by dissembling. The traditional virtues have disappeared and their place has been taken by a cynical realism: ". . . ex intimis praecordiis nunquam susceptae iniuriae memoriam obliterent, offensae vero livorem nusquam propalent, sed inserviant temporibus, simulando atque dissimulando."[80] In 1513 Machiavelli develops these theses systematically in his *Il Principe.*

The conclusions which Alberti draws are tragic: Momus confesses to Jupiter that during his stay on earth he has tried hard to come to a positive judgment about human history but has not succeeded in doing so. No human art—not even the art of war, which is the basis of human history coming to pass—offers the prerequisites for a happy life.[81] In war, the concern is neither for justice nor human greatness, every event is judged only by its success, the sight of the battles is frightening and they are occasioned only by the mad drive for power [Voluisse et regem fieri se, quod proxime ad deorum maiestatem regium imperium arbitraretur].[82]

So Alberti in *Momus* builds up to the famous speech of the tramp, his praise of the idler, who rejects every social duty. This speech is not—as some interpreters would have it—a grotesque and absurd eulogy of indolence. The praise of the idler is a possible consequence of the demythicizing of history. There are two possible approaches which can result from the recognition that history is a "mania." We can follow Erasmus in accepting mania as the only possible "ratio vivendi" and consequently claiming that life, thought and action have no meaning outside its precincts. That is why Erasmus urged people to affirm the theatre of the world and to delight in the spectacle. The masks which "Moria" gives to man are "translations" essential to living; by means of them we conceal a profound and tragic reality.

The second alternative is that which Alberti announces through his eulogy of the idler: there are some who cross the oceans, others who drain the seas, others again who drive tunnels through mountains. But the idler does not believe in the sense of any of these undertakings, he ignores history, he rejects delusion and prefers to renounce all possessions and commit himself to nothing: ". . . curis vacuus in quodcunque velis latus dulce obdormiscens nihil sperabat, nihil metuebat."[83] Because, as we realize, "social masks" are hollow, they must be rejected, and every social role denied, and it is no longer permissible to believe in the sacred fire of metaphorical and metamorphic human activity. For the idler every street corner is good enough to lie down on, as every possession is a burden and every social commitment a nightmare. While Erasmus' advice was to wear the mask of "mania," the thesis of the idler is radically negative, a refusal: "Nullum genus vitae se aiebat comperisse, quod quidem omni ex parte eligibilius appetibiliusque sit, quam eorum qui quidem vulgo mendicant, quos errones nuncupant."[84]

When Momus delivers his negative speech about human politics to Jupiter, Hercules, who is present, feels obliged to raise objections to it, to defend human ingenuity. But his defense is in vain: as he is speaking a terrible din is heard in the halls of Olympus: a huge triumphal arch—made of gold and silver votive pictures, dedicated by men in honor of the gods—collapses. The gods complain about the stench which arises from this human gift: the votive pictures are merely expressions of men's passions, which show themselves in pleas motivated by fear, hatred, envy, greed, and the like [aulas omnes caeli obscena tetraque odoris foeditatem et nausea complerant].

The conclusion drawn from the totality of Momus' experience appears in the fourth book: Alberti's considerations do not lead to a "reformation" of the theatre of the world [theatrum illud fabulis agendis factum], but to its tragic destruction. Momus hardly features any more. The gods revenge themselves by chaining him to a rock—he becomes a grotesque symbol of a Prometheus; and to what did his "unmaskings" and "criticisms" lead? Even his name, Momus, is ironically transformed to "Humus." The new protagonists of the fable are now Charon, who ferries the souls of the dead across Acheron far below the earth and who now emerges from the underworld for the first time to contemplate the wonders of nature, and the philosopher Gelastus, the ridiculous. In their speeches the traditional philosophers are again criticized, again we encounter satires of false religiousness,[85] a criticism of causal thinking as the basis of metaphysics (such as we find in Ficino), and discussions about politics: Alberti here uses the metaphor of the state as a ship that is constantly being attacked by pirates.

The book culminates in the destruction of the theatre of the world: a storm destroys the "world stage" on which human history is enacted. In the wake of this, what gods will remain on the earth and what tasks will still seem meaningful to men? Three gods survive the catastrophe on earth:

the goddess of Hope, the god of Wealth and the goddess of the Night. Hope stayed on earth because she broke a wing when the theatre of the world collapsed: she is therefore the only goddess left who can help men. Pluto, the god of wealth, did not succeed in fleeing the earth either, for men immediately pounced on him, greedy for his treasures: they even tore out his eyes, believing them to be jewels; so wealth runs blindly through the streets of Florence.

The third and last remaining goddess is the Night: she is of no help to men, but she rises up as a symbol of the rhythm of world history. Apollo, the god of the sun, of light, of harmony, is in love with Night, but he can never reach her because she hides with her daughter, the Shadow (*umbra* is feminine): "Noctis filia est Umbra, et eam quidem Apollo ita amat perdite, ut nusquam esse nisi Umbra comite didicerit."[86]

Light and darkness are therefore intimately joined, where one appears the other will also come forward. If peace and order are recognized as the goal of human history, in so far as they realize a supernatural order (in accordance with the traditional conception as we encountered it in Dante), and if, in contrast, war is seen as destruction, then Alberti's metaphor reveals human history as a necessary, unbroken concatenation of war and peace, chaos and order, from which ever new worlds arise. No order that has temporarily been achieved, no cosmos, has ever survived the times: attempting to preserve them means misunderstanding the meaning and rhythm of the self-revelation of being. He who will not recognise the regularity with which the world constantly unveils and conceals itself will himself come to a tragic end.

Alberti draws the following conclusion from this insight into the mission of man: he distinguishes good as such and evil as such and that which in itself is neither good nor evil. Admittedly, the text gives us no rational definition of these concepts; rather Alberti just points to the things through which they appear in various ways from time to time. Good results in ever new forms from industry, vigilance, diligence, accuracy and assiduousness [Industriam, Vigilantiam, Studium, Diligentiam, Assiduitatem].[87] Evil as such also takes on ever new shapes derived from envy, ambition, lust, indigence [Invidia, Ambitio, Voluptas, Desidia, Ignavia].[88] Finally he distinguishes that which in itself is neither good nor evil, such as wealth, honor, and all that man normally strives for: these gain meaning through the use (*usus*) man puts them to at any given time.

In *Momus* Alberti denies the possibility of any *a priori* knowledge; he criticizes the illusion of a possible reformation of the world. No abstract theory is valid: only vigilance and perseverence, rooted in "usus" and "experientia" and always regarding ever new tasks, are of decisive importance.

CHAPTER SIX

Antiplatonism and Platonism

1

The Problem of Non-Platonic Humanism

THE QUESTIONS OF THE HUMANIST TRADITION TO WHICH WE HAVE already referred—namely, the preeminence of metaphoric thought and discourse, the primacy of poetic language and the philosophical function of metaphor in its opposition to rational, defined thought—stand in contradiction not only to medieval discussions, but also to the problems of modern philosophy. Even today these questions influence speculative thought. Analytic philosophy still recognizes the danger of the metaphorical expressions found in everyday language, and in scientific research it endeavors to replace them with mathematical and abstract formulae. It is no mere chance when Hegel—who condemns metaphoric language as unphilosophical— nevertheless resorts to metaphors for his chapter headings in the *Phenomenology*: "The Unfortunate Conscience," "Master and Servant," etc.

The unceasing criticism of the "litterae" and their exclusion from the realm of philosophy (not only poetry, but also rhetoric, history and philology, from Descartes to the further development of modern thought) show how, even today, the problems which are closely connected with them cannot be dismissed. Even in the realm of German Idealism the word is accorded a philosophical function as a result of its "divine capacity to change the mind"—as Hegel puts it in the *Phenomenology*. When in this work, Hegel interprets the mysteries of Ceres and Bacchus in Eleusis and their corresponding rites, his interpretation is metaphorical. From this perspective it is not only historically, but also theoretically, important to interpret anew the significance of the theses of the Tübingen circle (Hölderlin, Schelling, Hegel) as to the role of the imagination. The so-called *Oldest Systematic Program of German Idealism,* which is attributed to Hegel[1] and which is also included in Hölderlin's complete works,[2] states expressly that poetry "will at the end once again be what it was at the beginning, the instructress of humanity; as there will be no more philosophy or history, poetry alone will supersede all the other sciences and arts."[3] The same fragment ends with the thesis: "Philosophy must become mythology in order to render the philosophers sensual."[4]

Before we refer briefly to the Platonic Humanist tradition, which has been discussed thoroughly enough in the history of philosophy, let us summarize the results of our interpretation of the non-Platonic tradition of Humanism. This tradition does not concern itself with the problem of the rational knowledge of being: such a starting point for philosophizing would—corresponding to the schemata of traditional metaphysics—imply the preeminence of rational thought, which encompasses the logic of causal reasoning. Instead, the Humanists proceed from the problem of the word, and, moreover, the word as belonging to that sphere in which the existential claim of Being is experienced. The primacy of the principles of philosophy reveals itself in the necessity of the claim which demands a response in the "here" and "now" of the "necessary" utterance; these principles can only be demonstrated, as Aristotle emphasizes, through "elenchic" procedures, not through rational proofs. He asserts that first principles can never be proved rationally (they have no apodictic character): their primacy is revealed by the fact that it is impossible to escape them. Hence Aristotle attributes an "elenchic" character to them. In the language of the earliest philosophy, ἐλέγχειν means to chain someone to the pillory in such a way that he is unable to free himself: the enchained is exposed to the ridicule of the crowd.[5] We are chained to the necessity of having to express ourselves—even in situations of meaningful silence, just as Prometheus was exposed on the rock and open to all attacks. With respect to the necessity of language, it is not by chance that we speak of the "being-exposed" in the "being-there."

The specific problem of Humanist philosophy, to which we have already referred, is how, when and through what mode of language "being-there" experiences the claim of Being, corresponding to Dante's assertion that language arises "vel per modum interrogationis vel per modum responsionis."[6] "Being-there" reveals itself in the existential necessity of language; first of all in the silent response of "being-there" to the claims of Being in the given situation, and then as the silence of Being breaks into language in response to the demand. That is, the "truth" of the word understood not as the rational correspondence to being ("adaequatio rei et intellectus," as expressed traditionally), but as ἀλήθεια, as the spoken disclosure of the claim of Being as it reveals itself in the given situation. Only in the primal sphere does the resorting to signs, to indicating movements, even to silence, attain meaning: outside of the claim everything is unresponsive and indeterminate, as in an impenetrable forest without "clearings."

Primal language reveals itself as one of "transference," as "metaphoric," for every disclosed being refers beyond itself to something else — to the addressed, which exists apart from it. The claim is unveiled through the disclosed being, and only then will it be simultaneously concealed in it. It is thus understandable that Humanism, when considering these problems, rejected the preeminence of a rational language which can only produce abstract, logical definitions of being that lie outside of any experience of "time" or "place," definitions unable to recognize the philosophical function of metaphor.

It follows that for Humanism each meaning of an expression that counts in logic as "essential" is "inessential," even though it has been defined rationally. What has validity in logic as "serious" discourse "lacks" that seriousness in the framework of the Humanist problematic. Even irony — which rhetoric defines as a metaphoric mode of expression, since it lets the actual meaning of a being appear through the reversal of its rational meaning in the context of discourse — attains here its basic philosophical recognition and function.

In summary, we might say that metaphor — inasmuch as it states something and means something else at one and the same time — appears to "invert" the principles of rational thought (those of contradiction, identity, the exclusion of the third party). The ironic expression, on the other hand, since it does not state what is determined rationally, but "reverses" it, becomes a new form of thought and discourse. Finally, when "rational discourse" claims to be the preeminent and hence original, "serious" mode of thought and speech, then it reveals itself as "lacking" in seriousness: its abstract nature exposes its inability to correspond to the claim of being

historically, i.e., in the "here" and "now." Only in light of this consciousness do the modes of thought and discourse in Poliziano's "Lamia," the
style of Erasmus' *Praise of Folly* and Alberti's *Momus,* and the meaning
of Valla's rhetoric become intelligible.

Humanism thus represents a complete reversal of the traditional medieval
conception of the relationship between philosophy and poetry. In the medieval conception truth is concealed under the veil of metaphor; in the Humanist tradition the situation is reversed: metaphor, poetry and irony disclose
what rational thought and discourse are unable to unveil. Again and again
metaphor, "pointing" but not "proving," gives notice of succeeding epochs:
thus men are amazed at the fact that the certainty of rational proof never
represents the final achievement of historical development. Existence reveals itself in this way as the realization of a mania, an "adventure." Metaphoric insight—the primal form of correspondence to the appeal which
presents itself "here" and "now"—produces, as a result of its character
as image, the structural pathos of "being-there," and so transcends the
duality of theory and praxis inasmuch as this always reveals itself in the
individual example.

We will now consider the Platonic tendency within Humanism, so it
becomes evident that this tendency not only distances itself from the previously discussed questions of non-Platonic Humanism, but is unable as well
to yield anything new which goes beyond the basic arguments of traditional philosophy.

2

The Problematic of Platonic Humanism

It has been the aim of our previous discussions to shed light on the
tradition of non-Platonic Humanism, which has until now never been
sufficiently recognized or evaluated. The authors to whom we have referred
have been studied principally by literary historians or Romanists, rarely
by historians of philosophy.

But the discovery of a specific problematic of Humanism implies a re-
vision of the traditional schema of the beginning of modern thought (usually
said to begin with Descartes, as in Heidegger's polemical rejection of Humanism), and of the identification of Humanism with Platonism. Neither anthro-

pology nor Platonism should be regarded as specifically new problems of Humanism; rather the question concerns the existential correspondence of the claim of Being, on the basis of which being arrives at meaning in various situations. This problem is resolved in and through the poetic word, not through a rational determination of what is given. The assertion of the preeminence of the existential situation, which finds its correspondence in the metaphorical "verbum," presupposes consciousness of the preeminence of poetic, metaphoric language; in accord with Pontano's formulation (*fatum* = fari), the word itself becomes man's fate.

The Platonic Humanist tradition distances itself radically from these problems. It proceeds from the problem of the rational definition of being, in accord with which knowledge endeavors to attain "surety" or "certainty" by anchoring these in abstraction, as universals, in the non-historical. Everything which is revealed through the senses appears as a reflection of "ideas," of the rational concepts which constitute the eternal cause of the appearance. The meaning of words is located in the logical transcendence of what the senses reveal; so man is raised through this rational process to a vision of the eternal, to being by and for itself. Philosophical Platonism, to which we now briefly turn, will scarcely add anything new from a philosophical standpoint to this traditional schema of metaphysical thought.

The Florentine Council of the fourteenth century, whose goal was the unification of the Greek and Roman churches, provided the occasion for a new western interest in Platonism. The Greek scholar Manuel Chrysoloras—who taught Greek at the Florentine "Studio" between 1397 and 1400—gave people the opportunity to read the classic texts in the original. Bruni notes in his chronicle that he turned to this study with such zeal that he dreamt while asleep of what he had learned by day.[7] The Greek philosopher Georgius Plethon (1355–1450) also sojourned in Florence. Cosimo de Medici, fired by his enthusiasm for Platonic thought, founded the Academy which bears Plato's name, and commissioned the still young Marsilio Ficino, son of his doctor, to translate and interpret the works of Plato. Cardinal Bessarion (1403–1472) and George of Trebizond (1395–1484) recognized that Platonic thought gave them the possibility of making an important contribution to Christian thought. Cardinal Bessarion translated Aristotle's *Metaphysics* and endeavored to bring Aristotelian and Platonic thought together in his *In Calumniatorem Platonis*.

In his inaugural lecture at the "Studio" in Florence in 1458, Cristoforo Landino asserts the preeminence of poetry among the seven liberal arts, yet in the end he remains anchored to Platonic thought. It is the task of the poet to reveal "divine" wisdom. In the fourth book of the *Camaldulensian Discourses* he maintains that the task of poetry is to express in sublime speech what is concealed in God: "tam maxime excelsa quaedam et in ipso divinitatis fonte recondita promant." And therefore poetry should never be seen as a mere game: "meras fabellas ad cessantium aures oblectandas ludere credantur."[8]

In order to indicate the importance of poetry he refers in his inaugural lecture to the fact that all the texts of Greek antiquity and the Judaic and the Christian writers make use of metaphoric language. "There were no historians in Greece when Homer portrayed the famous battles and the heroic age of the Trojans. There were no philosophers when the same poet gave instructions for leading an army, for ordering the state and for how to lead a proper life."[9] He repeats the thesis that the Romans were justified in calling the poets "vates," a definition which he derives from the "vi mentis," that is, from the power of the imagination.[10] Yet, under the influence of Platonic thought, poetry is legitimized in this discourse because it leads men back to that a-historical reality which constitutes the eternal principle of all human life: "rivolare all'antica patria."[11] "When the human soul lived in heaven," Landino continues, "it was part of the eternal divine spirit from which the movement and the order of the divine spheres derives; now that it is lost in the slime of the earth [terrestre limo], it can only free itself from the earthly shackles which hinder it through music and the order of poetry" [da terreni legami ritardato é l'animo].[12]

During the Renaissance, Platonism and Aristotelianism come to cover up the problems which we have observed in Humanism, and which lead to difficulties with Landino. We now proceed with a consideration of the *Theologica Platonica* of Marsilio Ficino (1433–1499). The basic premise of this work is the precedence assigned to the rational determination of being, which helps, through rational thought, to transcend becoming, the mutability of being and its relativity as they are experienced through the senses. Hence the goal which our author sets for himself: to explain the becoming of being by reference to a first cause as the highest being, as the primal cause (*ratio*). The schema of traditional ontological thought is adopted once more; it proceeds from a determination of matter. Matter is defined as being in itself, and its characteristic quality is tardiness (*pigritia*): "pigram hanc molem corporū."[13] The following mechanistic argument is called upon to give support: what is effective must possess strength, must be able to penetrate what is passive: "primum, ut agens in seipso potentissimum sit. Secundum, ut ad motum promptissimum. Tertium, ut facile penetret patiens, atque ipsum patiens agenti proxime uniatur."[14] Since substance or material is identified with the "moles corporum," it cannot bring forth any effect itself: "quanto magis augetur corpus, tanto magis retardat motum, ac differt diutius actionem."[15]

But if matter is passive, non-effecting, undifferentiated and indifferent being, how then can we refer to it? The solution which Ficino gives to this problem is indicative of the difficulties in which he finds himself: he asserts that matter is that being "which is most distant from first causes and which is most close to the abyss" [a primo esse distat longissime, atque est proxima nihilo].[16] It is that which makes the effecting impure, that which is an obstacle to it.

Since Ficino defines matter as non-effecting because of its structure, he refers back to the Aristotelian explanation of becoming: matter "becomes," "undergoes changes" through the varying forms, the figures which it assumes successively: "Sunt autem non per molem in specie hac aut illa, sed per hanc formam aut illam, per formam igitur operantur."[17] Form becomes effective through its character, its quality: "Qualitatem . . . omnem formam divisam in corpore appellamus . . . formae natura simplex, efficax, agilis ad agendum."[18] The becoming of being is explained by the fact that matter continually adopts new forms.

Ficino's admonition follows: one must distance oneself from matter, from its influence on characteristics and forms, as these represent the first stage of the effecting. Through their effectiveness the characteristics of forms represent a higher, less material mode of being: "Iam igitur a corpore ad qualitatem ascendimus."[19] As matter and form are joined together at this first stage of "coming into being," the effecting element remains "impure": it does not possess any distance from matter: "[forma] . . . ex agili fit inepta. Ideo neque mera forma haec est, neque vera, neque perfecta. Non potest haec prima forma esse, si mera non est."[20] The striving towards ever higher, purer stages of the effecting follows as a necessary consequence, until one arrives at the highest effective form: "Mens humana quotidie a particularibus formis ad universales absolutasque se confert."[21]

Ficino's goal can be summarized in his own words: "Let us transcend physical form and observe the first form which arises once we have distanced ourselves from material form. Physical form assumes the role of an inbetween stage; on the one hand, it possesses something material, as it extends into the material sphere, on the other hand, it is no longer some-thing merely physical, as it consists of both form and matter."[22]

Corresponding to the model of causal, mechanistic thought, Ficino as-serts the existence of a "first," effecting, primal being, God: "solum autem post mortem corporis beatior effici potest; necessarium esse videtur ani-mis nostris ab hoc *carcere* discedentibus lucem aliquam superesse."[23] The release from imprisonment presupposes that the world in which man lives belongs to the realm of the unreal, of illusion, of shadows. Hence his repeat-ed warning: "solvamus, obsecro, coelestes animi coelestis patriae cupidi, solvamus quamprimum vincula compedum terrenarum."[24]

Platonic Humanism directs its attention completely towards a rational definition of being according to causal explanation, i.e., each being has a cause, a first principle, and the first cause is identified with the first, highest being, God. Thus we remain within the confines of the traditional schema, which is of course quite different from the problematic we have developed so far.

Giovanni Pico della Mirandola (1463–1494) also confirms our thesis: his *Heptaplus* concerns the principle of an explanatory cause as the basis of philosophizing, and hence of causal, rational thought. This principle implies a first, effective being as the cause of the becoming of being. Once again, matter is defined as passive being in itself: ". . . materiam rudem, formarum expertem, idoneam quidem omnibus formis suscipiendis, sua tamen natura omnibus privatam."[25] Our author identifies rational thought with causal thought: "animus rationalis, a causis ad effectus se transfe-rens, rursusque ab effectibus recurrens in causas, ratiocinationis orbe circumvolvitur."[26] Correspondingly, he explains the creation of the world according to the Aristotelian schema of the becoming of being[27] and the creative activity of the artist.[28]

This model of thought makes it possible for Pico to strive after a "pure" world, not an "impure" one broken through becoming, a world from whose realm the relative and the ever-changing is excluded. Our author distin-guishes three worlds: the first, which is the realm of the "intelligible," the supra-sensual, and which constitutes the object of study of theologians and philosophers; the world of light and pure activity which derives from the spirit: "illic vita perpetua et stabilis operatio; in caelo vitae stabilitas . . . ex divina mentis natura."[29] The second world is the world of the planets which, because of its eternal movement, constitutes the certain, pure world: "duae partes ambae obtectae et undique ab omni peregrina iniuria liberae."[30] The third world is the realm which lies under the influence of the moon, where the "coming into being" of being is no longer whole or integral; in this sphere life and death follow one another, everything is in flux and continually changing: "Hic per aquas notatur, fluxa instabilique substantia."[31] The allegorical, metaphorical description of the world which transcends the realm of the sensual is legitimized through the causal "framework of relationships," that is, through the common factor which binds the three worlds together.[32]

In the *Heptaplus*, Pico asserts that the Aristotelian thesis of the four causes may be found in *Genesis* in a "veiled," metaphoric form: ". . . revocemus . . . fuisse veterum sapientum celebre institutum res divinas ut, aut plane non scriberent, aut scriberent dissimulanter."[33] This mode of speaking and writing is found among the ancient peoples,[34] e.g., Moses' expressions are visual, not conceptual: "When he refers to the first cause or to matter, he refers to heaven or earth."[35] We thus find here a concept of metaphor radically opposed to that of the Humanist tradition to which we have already referred. The rational causality of being joins together the various stages of being and constitutes the "common factor" which permits the use of analogy.

In *De dignitate hominis* Pico locates man exclusively within the framework of traditional ontology; the problems which arise out of this location do not lead to any "new" advances in thought. Man contains within himself all that is given in nature [omnium in se naturarum substantias et totius universitatis plenitudinem re ipsa complectitur];[36] he represents a microcosm of being inasmuch as he brings together within himself the vegetable life of the plants, the sensible life of the animals, and the faculty of "reason," which contains the image of God.[37]

The "dignitas" of man as a living being – as opposed to all other beings – is constituted by the fact that he, from the beginning, has no definite form: "hominem accepit indiscretae opus imaginis."[38] As an individual being he himself can choose his own form: "pro tuo arbitrio, in cuius manu te posui."[39] "I have made you neither as a heavenly nor as an earthly being, neither as immortal nor as mortal, so that you, following your own initiative, that is, as the creator of your own self, can take on the form which you choose for yourself."[40] From Pico's emphasis on individual being the thesis follows that nature "is placed at man's disposal"[41] as the given object of human activity.

In our observations on non-Platonic Humanism we have emphasized the experience of the existential claim with respect to the word which reveals the world, an experience which Erasmus defines as "folly," as "moria." For the Platonist Pico, just as for Ficino in his treatise on love, "moria" is understood in the sense of the Platonic "furor," "mania," which is interpreted as the experience of the divine—that passive experience which transports man beyond the realm of the historical in order to lead him back to the realm of the primal, the transcendent: ". . . agemur Socraticis furoribus, qui extra mentem ita nos ponant, ut mentem nostram et nos ponant in Deo."[42]

In no way does Platonic Humanism go beyond the boundaries of traditional speculative thought, and so it leads us to no "new" insights. L. F. Cattani (1466–1522), known as "Diacceto" after the name of the place of his birth, also focusses in his philosophy on the problem of being as it is mediated to us through the senses. From the very beginning he asserts that physical being in itself can lay no claim to truth: this is obvious because of its continual becoming and changing. The cause is impure substance, whose characteristic is defined through its "suffering" quality, through its passivity, and which assumes its "form" only through interaction with the effecting causes.[43] In *De pulchro*[44] he maintains that everything in the realm of matter is false since only contradiction, struggle and dissolution can be demonstrated here.[45] Matter is the realm of asymmetry; it has no unity and everything in it comes and goes;[46] there is no truth to be found because everything "becomes" without having any "permanent being"; whereas the characteristic of the true is constancy.[47] Matter "takes shape" through the ordering forces which are revealed in the cosmos.

From all this Diacceto concludes that we must admit that heaven and earth represent the pillars of the Gods, which are formed from a sublime substance and through a marvelous art and which must be honored more than any other representation of the divinity.[48] The totality of the universe, with its linking of cause and effect, is understood as an emanation of divine being: "Just as the universe rises above all bodies, without excluding a single one of them, so it is necessary that it possess a sublime spirit and a body from which are derived all individual souls, and through which everything participates in an omnipotent intelligence."[49] For Diacceto there also exist various stages of being: that of the natural elements, which do not move themselves but which are moved through others, and (corresponding to the Aristotelian schema) fire and air, which move upwards, and earth and water, which move downwards. Then there are the bodies which move of their own volition as the result of the principle we call spirit: plants, which possess the ability to take nourishment, and animals, who have the ability to distinguish between pleasure and pain. Moving on, there are human beings, who approximate the understanding of angels in that they strive towards the transcendent; finally, there is the highest being.

If we now proceed to compare Platonic Humanism with the tradition to which we have already referred, it becomes clear that the latter has "reversed" the whole of the speculative tradition. "Usus" and "experimentia" replace the *a priori* idea; the question of the existential claim replaces the problem of causal, rational thought; the investigation of the word as the correspondence of the existential claim takes the place of the rational definition of being; the assertion of the preeminence of metaphoric language over rational language is maintained. We are thus obliged to recognize not only the need to revise the traditional schema according to which Humanism is interpreted, but we must also rethink the historical schema according to which the beginning of modern thought is equated with the rationalism of Descartes.

3

Conclusion and Perspective:
Humanist Theses and Idealist Romantic Philosophy

We have continually referred to the speculative content of that tradition which became the model for Western thought. Following Plato's interpretation of Socratic thought, the principal problem became the question of the rational definition of being, that is, the "causal understanding," the explanation of its essence, its οὐσία. This led to a definition (χωρισμός), a determination of being independent of "time" and "space." And the definition of manifold being through rational, causal thought led to the definition of the "first," primal being—God: an onto-theological metaphysics in which the problem of being had precedence over that of the word. From Plato onwards the "idea" (the basis of the definition of the given being, and hence of rational thought) is central to philosophy: the a-historical becomes the highest goal of metaphysics.

Contemporary analytic philosophy, however, with its denial of the possibility of metaphysics, leads to the fundamental concept of science as pure formalism: this results from its basic denial of any philosophical meaning of rhetoric and poetry, and hence the Humanist tradition. Can philosophy in the sense of traditional metaphysics, or of purely "logical," "rational," "formal" analytic thought, still provide any answer to contemporary problems in the area of speculative thought?

The "Humanist" tradition, which we have discussed here,[50] does not proceed from the problem of being and its rational definition, but from the problem of the word as it is experienced in existential situations. The word itself is the primary mode of experiencing the claim of being in the historical situation, and this claim can neither be located nor answered through any rational definition of being.

Primal metaphoric thought and discourse do not therefore result from the "inventio" of what is held in common between linguistic expressions; rather they consist of discovering what exists in common between the claimant and that which finds a correspondence to it through the interpreting word. The "claim" is first unveiled – and simultaneously concealed – when each interpretation of being refers to the claimant, which then covers up the given being, and hence conceals existence in the "here" and "now": that is, through metaphoric language.

Following our discussion of the non-Platonic philosophy of Humanism, it becomes evident that analytic philosophy, because of its pure "formality," can make no statements as to how we realize our existence. But the theses of Humanism, those which concern the philosophical function of ingenious, metaphoric, poetic and rhetorical language, do lay claim to being able to provide essential insights into the questions of our existence. The problems of existence only have meaning in the concrete sphere of the responses to the claims which not only become apparent to us in the given situation, but which also demand our attention. Purely "formal" discussions, for example those of analytic philosophy, which ignore the concrete appeal in which man as he exists finds himself, and traditional metaphysics, with its a-historical concerns, can yield no answer. They can neither ask nor answer the essential questions.

And the Humanist tradition is not only "newly" evaluated and thought through in its whole frame of reference by Vico, it continues to influence Gracian,[51] Thesauro and Pellegrini in the eighteenth century, as can be seen in their discussions of "ingenium" and "acumen." The same problems are discussed once more in Germany in the Romanticism of Novalis, the Schlegel brothers and Schelling, and in England in Shaftesbury's discourse *Sensus Communis, An Essay of Freedom of Wit and Humour* and in Coleridge's *Biographia Literaria* in the nineteenth century. Hegel's *Outline of the Oldest Systematic Program of German Idealism* (1797–1799), to which we have already referred, contains a number of basic Humanist theses. From our discussion of Humanism the question therefore arises as to whether the theses of Idealist Romantic Philosophy might not be interpreted anew and as to whether new approaches to philosophy might not arise out of this connection.

The passage from the *Systematic Program* which represents the decisive statement of the philosophical importance of poetic, and hence of metaphoric thought and discourse, reads as follows: "The philosopher must possess as much aesthetic imagination as the poet. Men without aesthetic sense are our bread and butter philosophers . . . . At this point it is evident as to what those men lack who do not understand ideas – and who admit honestly that everything remains in the dark for them the moment matters go beyond tables and registers. Poetry, however, is accorded a higher dignity, and at the end it will become once again what it was at the beginning – the teacher of humanity; then there will be neither philosophy nor history. Poetry alone will remain and it will survive art. . . . We shall have to have a new mythology, but this mythology will serve ideas, it will be a mythology of reason. Mythology must become philosophical in order to make philosophy sensual."[52]

Setting aside the historical question as to which of the German Idealists (Hegel, Hölderlin or Schelling) was responsible for the thesis, we may say that Hegel obviously aims to draw a basic distinction: he contrasts the tradition of the philosophical function and meaning of poetic and metaphoric thought and discourse and the tradition of purely rational and formal thought and discourse. There will be a movement from the philosophy of the rational and abstract to a concrete philosophy that arises as a response to the claims man faces in the "here" and "now."

Do the theses which are contained in the earliest version of the *Systematic Program of German Idealism* – with their positive emphasis on poetry and rhetoric – culminate in a problematic which is theoretically and historically vital today? Only when we become conscious of the historical and theoretical importance of this question, and when our research makes reference to it, will we be able to assess the problems of Humanism and of

German Idealism, and so become able to define thoroughly the new philosophical problems which lie before us. To what degree can the theses of the "Idealist System" fragment be understood in light of the specific Humanist tradition of the fifteenth century in its whole frame of reference?

As we have discussed, the meaning of an expression defined rationally in logic as the "actual" meaning is a "false" meaning in the Humanist tradition – precisely because of its abstract, a-historical meaning. And, likewise, in traditional metaphysics every metaphoric expression counts as "false" since it does not meet logical standards. Thus, Humanist philosophy expresses an "inverted" thought for the thought of traditional metaphysics. Metaphor – inasmuch as it asserts something and means something else at the same time, and so goes beyond the principles of rational logic, with its corresponding thought and discourse – "inverts" traditional philosophy. For example, an "ironic" expression, which does not state what can be rationally defined, but "reverses" it, becomes, with the Humanists or the German Idealists, a new form of thought and discourse.

This problematic is found in Novalis, Jean Paul and the Schlegel brothers, all following Schelling's thesis on the philosophical function of poetry. The preeminence of ingenious activity – which consists in the "finding" (*inventio*) of relationships, of "similtudines," which constitute the foundation of rhetoric and metaphoric poetic thought and discourse – gains new meaning in these Romantic writers. The theoretical problem underlying the Romantic thesis of the "inverted" world and the "inverted mode of thought and speech" (about which both Hegel and Tieck speak, if in different ways), and hence of the speculative meaning of irony and wit, arises anew.

Novalis asserts: "Wit is creative – it produces 'similarities' ";[53] and Friedrich Schlegel states: "Wit, *ars combinatoria*, criticism, ingenuity are *all one and the same*."[54] Elsewhere, he refers to the "ingenious and simultaneously ordering and combining function" of wit.[55] And with respect to Vico's and Gracian's definition of the philosophical meaning of ingenium, we should also mention Schlegel's thesis that wit and memory are closely connected to one another. Wit arises out of an original unity, the imaginative power of being able to uncover analogies and similarities in the fragmentary world. "Without any relationship to what has preceded, wit emerges completely unexpectedly, suddenly, as if a deserter, or rather as a flash from the subconscious world."[56]

Schlegel can also claim, *as opposed* to the systematic procedure of understanding and reason, that the method of wit "parallels the process of being born,"[57] and in such a manner that it reveals itself as an "ars inveniendi." He expressly identifies wit with the traditional structure and procedure of ingenious activity. Wit, in its combinatory capacity, enables one "to find similarities which are otherwise independent, different and separate, but which bring to unity the most heterogeneous and the most different elements."[58] Wit is revealed as the expression which, through its ingenious activity, creates order out of the fullness of dissimilar elements, and which is able to give form to chaos by realizing a basic urge.

In connection with the fundamental thesis as to the preeminence of poetic language and its philosophical function, we should also remember that August Wilhelm Schlegel asserts the following in his *Berlin Lectures on Poetry and Art* of 1801, that is, shortly after the *Outline of German Idealism*: "Men seek in and through poetry either an outer cover for something spiritual or they relate something external to an invisible core."[59]

Jean Paul's *Introduction to Aesthetics* (1804) also discusses the problem of "wit" in connection with that of "perspicacity" (for Vico, *acutezza*, for Gracian, *agudeza*) and that of insight: "Wit 'creates' (*inventio*) similarities from what is dissimilar, even from among distinctly different factors, whereas perspicacity finds dissimilarities between similar elements and insight finds complete similarity."[60] Regarding the problem of symbolism, John Neubauer of the University of Pittsburgh has justly stated that knowledge of Schelling's *System of Transcendental Idealism*[61] must be presupposed in order to understand Schlegel's thesis of the philosophical function of poetry.[62]

What clearly arises out of the preceding theoretical discussions is the necessity not only of interpreting and understanding anew the "ingenious" character of wit, irony and the "inverted mode" (as opposed to purely rational philosophy), but also of researching again the historical relationships between the theses of Humanism and those of Romantic Idealism. Our resort to "indicating" sounds, signs, movements, even silence, has meaning only in the primal sphere of that which "makes claims" on us from the abyss: beyond the claim everything is silent, indeterminate, as in a primal forest without "clearings," without a "theatrical stage" for history.

Notes

NOTES

Notes to the Introduction

1. B. Spaventa, *Della filosofia italiana nelle sue relazioni con la filosofia europea* (Bari, 1913), p. 31; on this debate between Italian and German philosophy, cf. E. Grassi, *Vom Vorrang des Logos* (München: Beck, 1939).

2. Martin Heidegger, *Hölderlins Hymne "Der Ister"* (Frankfurt a. M.: Vittorio Klostermann, 1984), p. 86; my emphasis.

3. Heidegger, p. 191.

4. Heidegger, p. 155.

5. Heidegger, p. 106 and 98.

6. Heidegger, p. 102; my emphases.

7. Martin Heidegger, *Platons Lehre von der Wahrheit. Mit einem Brief über den Humanismus* (Bern: Verlag A. Franck, 1947).

Notes to Chapter 1

1. René Descartes, *Regulae ad directionem ingenii*, Reg. III; *Discours de la méthode*, I, 8.

2. *Regulae*, IV, I.

3. G. Hegel, *Vorlesungen über die Geschichte der Philosophie*, ed. H. Glockner (Stuttgart, 1928), XVII, p. 59.

4. Hegel, XVIII, p. 427.

5. Hegel, XVIII, p. 419.

6. Hegel, XIX, p. 219.

7. Hegel, XVII, p. 121.

8. Hegel, XVII, p. 127.

9. Hegel, XVII, p. 149.

10. Mommsen, *Römische Geschichte* (Berlin, 1933), III, p. 619.

11. Mommsen, p. 620.

12. E. R. Curtius, "Neuere Arbeiten über den italienischen Humanismus," *Bibliothèque d'Humanisme et Renaissance* 9/10 (1947–48), p. 188.

13. E. Cassirer, *Individuum und Kosmos* (1927; rpt., Darmstadt: Wissenschaftliche Buchgesellschaft, 1963), p. 2.

14. E. Cassirer, *Das Erkenntnisproblem* (Leipzig/Berlin: Verlag Bruno Cassirer, 1922), p. 74.

15. K. O. Apel, *Transformation der Philosophie I: Sprachanalytik, Semiotik, Hermeneutik* (Frankfurt, 1976), p. 154.

16. P. O. Kristeller, *Humanismus und Renaissance* (München: Wilhelm Fink, 1974), I, p. 17.

17. W. Jaeger, "Antike und Humanismus," *Humanismus*, ed. H. Opperman (Darmstadt, 1970), p. 22.

18. Martin Heidegger, *Platons Lehre*, p. 62.

19. *Platons Lehre*, p. 63.

20. *Platons Lehre*, p. 75.

21. "Verum, quia omnis veritas que non est principium ex veritate alicuius principii fit manifesta, necesse est in qualibet inquisitione habere notitiam de principio, in quod analetice recurratur pro certitudine omnium propositionum que inferius assummuntur." Dante, *De monarchia*, a cura di Pier Giorgio Ricci = vol. 5 of *Le opere* . . . Edizione Nazionale (Milano: Mondadori, 1965), I, 2, p. 137.

22. Aristotle, *Metaphysics*, XII, 1069a 32.

23. *Met.* VI, 1026a 10.

24. "Potest enim rationabilis anima intra semetipsam de liberalibus disciplinis tractare, absque vocis articulatae disertaeque orationis strepitu." Johns Scotus, *De Divisione Naturae*, Lib. V, 4. *Patrologia Latina*, ed. J. Migne, vol. 122, p. 870.

25. ". . . non de rerum natura tractare videntur, sed vel de regulis humanae vocis . . ." J. Scotus, p. 869 D.

26. Bonaventure, *I. Sententiarum*, Dist. XXII, Quaest. II.

27. Robert Grosseteste, *De Libero Arbitrio*, ed. L. Baur, in *Beiträge zur Geschichte der Philosophie des Mittelalters* (Münster, 1912), p. 191.

28. *De Monarchia*, I, 4, 1–2, p. 142 (emphasis mine).

29. Dante, *De vulgari eloquentia*, tr. Warman Welliver (Ravenna: Longo Editore, 1981), I, IX, p. 63.

30. Dante, *Il Convivio*, ed. G. Busnelli and G. Vandelli (Firenze: Felice le Monnier, 1968), I, XIII, 4, p. 83.

31. *Convivio*, I, XII, 1, p. 75–76.

32. *De vulgari eloquentia*, I, XVII, 2, p. 80 (emphases mine).

33. ". . . id cardinale vocetur. Nam sicut totum hostium cardinem sequitur ut, quo cardo vertitur, versetur et ipsum, seu introrsum seu extrorsum flectatur, sic et universus municipalium grex vulgarium vertitur et revertitur, movetur et pausat secundum quod istud . . ." *De vulgari eloquentia*, I, 18, 1, p. 82.

34. *De vulgari eloquentia*, I, XVIII, 2, p. 82.

35. *De vulgari eloquentia*, I, XVIII, 3, p. 82.

36. *De vulgari eloquentia*, I, XVIII, 4, p. 84.

37. ". . . curialitas nil aliud est quam librata regula eorum que peragenda sunt." *De vulgari eloquentia*, p. 84.

38. ". . . e questa grandezza dò io a questo amico, in quanto quello elli di bontade avea in podere e occulto, io lo fo avere in atto e palese nel la sua propria operazione, che è manifestare conceptua sentenza." *Convivio*, I, X, 9, p. 63.

39. *Convivio*, I, III, 4–5, p. 21.

40. Plato, *Phaedrus*. I have used the Loeb translation by H. M. Fowler (Cambridge, MA: Harvard Univ. Press, 1960), p. 511.

41. A. Mussato, *Tragoediae duae, Eclogae et Fragmenta, Epistolae*, Lugduni Batavorum.

42. "Per me Dardanii referuntur Pergama Teucri, quam fuerit Troiae Dardanus, *ante fui*." *Epist.* VII, 45 C.

43. "Utque viret Laurus semper, nec fronde caduca carpitur, aeternum sic habet illa decus. Inde est, ut Vatum cingantur tempora Lauro." *Epist.* IV, 41 C.

44. *Epist. Fratris Johannini*, 57 C: "Corona est circularis undique recedens a medio. . . . Poetica maxime circa varietates circuit, et versatur, et a medio veritatis ut plurimum elongatur."

45. *Epist.* XVIII, 61 A: "Fuit a primis Ars ista Theologia mundi."

46. *Epist.* IV, 40 F: "Grande ministerium nescit, Charissime, nescit."

47. *Epist.* IV, 41 A.

48. *Epist.* XVIII, 60 E.

49. "Interdum sacrae refero monimenta Minervae, incidit officiis atque Venus apta meis." *Epist.* VII, 44 B.

50. "Poesis, altera quae quondam Theologia fuit." *Epist.* VII, 44 C.

51. *Epist.* XVIII, 56 B.

52. *Metaphysics*, 1028a 10.

53. Francisco Petrarca, "Oratio laudis poeticae." in Carlo Godi, "La 'Collatio laureationis' del Petrarca," *Italia medioevale e umanistica*, XIII, 1970, p. 14.

54. ". . . vulgaria oportet linquere sub pedibus." Petrarca, *Epist. a Zoilo*, I

in *Poesie minori del Petrarca* (Milano: Dalla Società Tipografia Di Classici Italiana, 1831), III, p. 230.

55. ". . . magnum hinc subsistere nullum/Censuit ingenium, nisi sit dementia mixta." *Epist. a Zoilo*, p. 230.

56. "Ora forent quasi muta hominum, si spiritus orbi/Deforet Aonius." *Epist. a Zoilo*, p. 232.

57. Petrarch, *Africa*, IX, v. 90.

58. Petrarch, *Oratio*, p. 20, 9.

59. "Scripturum iecisse prius firmissima veri fundamenta decet." *Africa*, IX, v. 92–93.

60. ". . . non ille poete nomine censendus, nec vatis honore, sed uno nomine mendacis." *Africa*, IX, v. 103.

61. *Oratio*, p. 20–21, 9.

62. *Africa*, IX, 93–94.

63. "Mulceat exterius tantum, alliciatque tuentes." *Epist. a Zoilo*, I, p. 228.

64. *Oratio*, p. 21, 9.

65. "Quesitu asperior quo sit sententia, verum dulcior inventu." *Africa*, IX, 96.

66. "Volle lo Spirito Santo mostrare nel nubo verdissimo, nel quale Mosè vide, quasi come una fiamma ardente, Iddio." Giovanni Boccaccio, *Genealogia Deorum*, pp. 553–650 in *Trattatello in laude di Dante*, ed. P. G. Ricci (Milano: Ricardo Ricciardi Editore, 1965); the quotation appears on p. 618.

67. Boccaccio, p. 621.

68. Boccaccio, XIV, IX, p. 620; the quote is from Isidore.

69. ". . . mentem in desiderium dicendi compellere." Boccaccio, XIV, 7.

70. ". . . ex Dei gremio originem ducere, et ab effectu nomen assumere." Boccaccio, XIV, 7, p. 946.

Notes to Chapter 2

1. Leonardo Bruni, "In Commentaria primi belli Punici," *Humanistisch–Philosophische Schriften*. Ed. Hans Baron (Leipzig/Berlin: B. G. Teubner, 1928), p. 122.

2. A. Birkenmajer, "Der Streit des Alonso von Cartagena mit Leonardo Bruni Aretino. Vermischte Untersuchungen zur Geschichte der mittelalterlichen Philosophie." *Beiträge zur Geschichte der Philosophie des Mittelalters* XX, 5 (Münster: 1922), p. 175.

3. "Nihil est enim in rerum natura, cuius nos non in aliis rebus possimus uti vocabulo et nomine. Unde enim simile duci potest-potest autem ex omnibus-, indidem verbum unum, quod similitudinem continet, tralatum lumen adferet orationi." Birkenmajer, III, XL, 161.

4. L. Bruni, "Prefatio in Orationes Demosthenis," *Schriften*, p. 128.

5. L. Bruni, *Epistularum Libri* VIII (Florentiae, 1741), II, p. 108.

6. Bruni, Epist. II, *Schriften*, p. 236.

7. "... in rebus agendis celeritas et agilitas, animique magnitudo rebus sufficiens." L. Bruni, "Oratio in funere Nannis Strozae," *Stephani Baluzzi Miscellaneorum liber Tertius* (Parisiis, 1680), p. 231.

8. L. Bruni, "Ad Petrum Paulum Istrum Dialogus," *Beiträge zur Geschichte und Literatur der Italienischen Gelehrten renaissance II*, ed. Th. Klette (Greifswald: Julius Ubel 1889), pp. 39–84; I cite p. 49.

9. *Dialogus*, p. 44.

10. *Dialogus*, p. 44.

11. "ingenii acumen," *Dialogus*, p. 56.

12. "... facultatem ingenii tarditas precludat." "In nebulonem maledicum," *Nicolò Niccoli*, ed. G. Zippel (Firenze, 1890), p. 84.

13. Bruni, "De Studiis et litteris," *Schriften*, p. 8.

14. *Dialogus*, p. 44 (emphasis mine).

15. "De studiis," *Schriften*, p. 11.

16. "De studiis," *Schriften*, p. 19.

17. *Dialogus*, p. 50.

18. "Le rite di Dante e di Petrarca," *Schriften*, p. 61.

19. *Ep.* I, p. 79.

20. "Vita Aristotelis," *Schriften*, p. 47.

21. "De studiis," *Schriften*, p. 7.

22. "De studiis," *Schriften*, p. 19.

23. *Ep.* II, p. 156.

24. *Ep.* II, p. 135.

25. Cicero, *De finibus* I, 20, *Opera quae supersunt omnia* (London: Williams and Norgate, 1845), vol IV, p. 93; *De deorum natura* II, 23., vol. IV, p. 417.

26. "De studiis," *Schriften*, p. 13.

27. A. Poliziano, *Le Selve e la Strega*, per cura di Isidoro del Lungo (Firenze: G. C. Sansoni 1925), p. 184.

28. Poliziano, p. 226.

29. G. Hegel, *Werke*, ed. Glockner (Stuttgart, 1927), XII, p. 538.

30. *Werke*, p. 533.

31. Quintilian, *Institutiones*, 9. 2. 46; tr. Jean Cousin (Paris: Societe d'edition "Les Belles Lettres," 1978), Tome V, p. 193.

32. *Inst.* 8. 6. 1–4; Cicero, *Brutus* 17. 69.

33. Cicero, *De oratore* 3, 38, 152. *Opera*, vol. 1, p. 322.

34. Herodotus I, 64; Loeb translation by A. D. Godley (Cambridge, MA: Harvard, 1966), p. 74; Thucydides *History*, I, 134. 4.

35. Quintilian, *Inst.* 8. 6. 54.

36. *Inst.* 10. 1. 130, Tome VI, p. 106.

37. *Inst.* 5. 8. 3, Tome III, p. 121.

38. Aristotle, *Poetics* 1459a 7–8.
39. *Poetics*, 1459a 7–8.
40. Aristotle, *Rhetoric* 1411b 9 ss.
41. *Iliad* XI, 574; Aristotle, *Rhetoric* 1412a 1.
42. *Rhetoric* 1365a 32.
43. *Poetics* 1457b 6.
44. *Rhetoric* 1412a 13.
45. *Rhetoric* 1411b 11.
46. *Rhetoric* 1411b 12.
47. "oculos exemptiles," Poliziano p. 184.
48. ". . . cum satis inspectarunt, recondunt in theca," Poliziano, p. 184.
49. ". . . circumspectatque singula, scrutatur, indagat . . .," Poliziano, p. 186.
50. Poliziano, p. 186.
51. Poliziano, p. 186.
52. Poliziano, p. 228.
53. Poliziano, p. 186 (emphasis mine).
54. Poliziano, p. 188.
55. Poliziano, p. 202.
56. ". . . animas nostras, in corpora tanquam in carcerem coniectas." Poliziano, p. 208.
57. Poliziano, p. 218.
58. Poliziano, p. 220.
59. Poliziano, p. 220 (emphasis mine).
60. ". . . nimis brevi gyro grammaticum sepsit." Poliziano, p. 220.
61. Salutati, *De laboribus Herculis*, ed. B. L. Ullman (Zürich: Artemis-Verlag, 1951). 2 vols.
62. Salutati, I, 1, p. 3.
63. "parvi pendere, tum damnare," Salutati, I, 1, p. 3
64. Salutati, I, 1, p. 3.
65. "scientiam quaerere," Salutati, I, 9, p. 44.
66. Salutati, I, 9, p. 43.
67. Salutati, I, 9, p. 43 (emphasis mine).
68. Salutati, I, 9, p. 44 (emphasis mine).
69. Salutati, I, 9, p. 44.
70. "Taliam . . . germina ponentem." Salutati, I, 9, p. 44.
71. Salutati, I, 9, p. 44.
72. "quasi 'multa memorantem,' " Salutati, I, 9, p. 44.
73. Salutati, I, 9, p. 44.
74. Salutati, I, 9, p. 44.
75. Salutati, I, 9, p. 44.
76. Cicero, *De oratore* II, 38, *Opera*, I, 251.

77. Cicero, *De oratore* II, 38, 157, *Opera*, V. 1, p. 251.

78. Cicero, *Tusc. disput*, III, 1, *Opera* IV, p. 274; *De finibus*, V, 18, *Opera*, vol. IV, 194.

79. Cicero, *De inventione* I, 30, 49, *Opera*, I, p. 109.

80. Quintilian, *Inst. orat.* 10, 1, 130. *Opera*, VI, p. 106.

81. G. B. Vico, *The New Science*, Book II, V, [Kap. V] rvsd. tr. of Third Edition (1744) by Thomas Goddard Bergin and Max Harold Fisch. (Ithaca: Cornell U. P.), 1968.

82. ". . . quod ipsos id fecerit opinari cuius contrarium visibiliter percepissent." Salutati, I, p. 8.

83. Salutati, II, p. 587.

84. ". . . ut per illum omnia et in illo omnia que animalia dicimus esse dicantur." Salutati, II, p. 587.

85. "Ut nemini dubium videri debeat etiam in tanta deorum multitudine poetas non de pluribus sed de uno sensisse, sed eundem deum *pro varietate officiorum, temporum*, et *locorum* diversimodis nuncupasse." Salutati, II, p. 588. (emphasis mine)

86. Vico, *Elements* XLIX, p. 74.

87. Vico, p. 116.

88. Giovanni Pontano, "Aegidius," *Dialoge*, tr. Hermann Kiefer (München: Wilhelm Fink Verlag, 1984), p. 570.

89. "Aegidius," p. 570.

90. "Aegidius," p. 570.

91. "Aegidius," p. 570–572.

92. "Aegidius," p. 572.

93. "Aegidius," p. 574.

94. "Aegidius," p. 572.

95. "Aegidius," p. 572.

96. "Aegidius," p. 578.

97. "Aegidius," p. 578.

98. "Antonius,"in *Dialoge*, p. 178.

99. "Actius," p. 500.

100. *Aeneid* III, 570.

101. "Antonius," p. 176.

102. "Antonius," p. 176.

103. "Antonius," p. 180.

104. "Antonius," p. 180.

105. "Antonius," p. 182.

106. "Antonius," p. 188.

107. ". . . qua commotus ammiratione atque a portu aversus . . . ab auditu coepit," "Antonius," p. 178.

108. "Antonius," p. 178.

109. "Mythos synkeitai ex thaumasion," Aristotle, *Metaphysics* I, 2, 982b 12.

110. Pontano, "Actius," p. 508.

111. "Aegidius," p. 528–530.

112. ". . . primi poetae sacerdotes vocati . . .," "Actius," p. 510.

113. "Actius," p. 510.

114. "Actius," p. 510.

115. ". . . e silvis homines eruisti atque e speluncis." "Actius," p. 510.

116. "Actius," p. 510.

117. ". . . poetarum figuras lineamentaque." "Antonius," p. 188.

118. ". . . de *scriptorum ingeniis* deque scriptis ipsis sententiam ferre didicisses." "Antonius," p. 194.

119. Augustine, *De Civitate Dei* I, 14, *Patriologia Latina* VII, p. 29.

120. ". . . spes tamen cepit fore ut, antequam a vobis emigrem, Latinam videam philosophiam et cultu maiore verborum et elegantia res suas explicantem . . ." "Aegidius," p. 592.

121. ". . . ut ratio habeatur rerum, temporum, personarum, locorum . . ." "Aegidius," p. 602.

122. ". . . ut a primis eloquentiae cultoribus mutuata antiquissimisque dicendi magistris." "Actius," p. 438.

123. "Actius," p. 496.

124. "Actius," p. 498.

125. "Actius," p. 498.

126. "Aegidius," p. 552.

127. "Aegidius," p. 602.

128. "Aegidius," p. 552.

129. "Actius," p. 422.

130. ". . . historia . . . partibus constat e duabus, hoc est rebus et verbis." "Actius," p. 468.

131. "Actius," p. 468.

132. "Actius," p. 468.

133. "Actius," p. 468.

134. "Actius," p. 470.

135. "Actius," p. 470.

136. "Actius," p. 434.

137. "Actius," p. 488 (emphasis mine).

138. "Actius," p. 488.

139. "Actius," p. 432.

140. "Actius," p. 434.

141. "Actius," p. 494.

142. "Actius," p. 488.

143. "Actius," p. 422.
144. "Actius," p. 420.
145. "Actius," p. 422.

Notes to Chapter 3

1. Isidore of Seville, *Etymologiae* III, 18, *Patrologia Latina* vol. 82, p. 163.

2. "quod artis praeceptis regulisque consistat." Isidore, I, 1, p. 74.

3. Adelard of Bath, *De eodem et diverso* IV, 1. 25, *Beiträge zur Geschichte der Philosphie des Mittelalters* IV, 1, p. 27.

4. Isidore, I, XL, 1, p. 122.

5. Aristotle, *De Anima*, 429a 3.

6. Richard of St. Victor, *De Gratia Contemplationis* II, XVII, *Patrologia Latina* vol. 196, p. 96 A.

7. Boethius, *De musica* V, 1., *Patrologia Latina*, vol. 63, p. 1285.

8. Bonaventure, *In I Sententiarum*, Dist. XXII, Quaestio II.

9. Hrabanus Maurus, *De universo* XXII, II, *Patrologia Latina*, vol. CXI, p. 419 C.

10. Bernardus Silvestris, *The Commentary on the First Six books of the Aeneid of Vergil Commonly Attributed to Bernardus Silvestris.* Ed. Julia Ward Jones and Elizabeth Francis Jones (Lincoln: University of Nebraska Press, 1977), p. 3.

11. Scotus Eriugena, *De Divisione Naturae*, V, *PL.* 122, p. 869 D.

12. Guarino Veronese, *Epistolario*, ed. R. Sabbadini, III vols. (Venezia, 1915–1919): Ep. 213 (I, 341), 50.

13. Veronese, Ep. 4 (I, 8), 26.

14. Veronese, Ep. 148 (I, 244), 24.

15. Veronese, Ep. 150 (I, 247), 13.

16. Veronese, Ep. 150 (I, 247), 15.

17. Veronese, Ep. 257 (I, 402), 12, Cf. also Ep. 477 (I, 669), 19.

18. Veronese, Ep. 377 (I, 544), 16.

19. Veronese, Ep. 803 (II, 478), 80.

20. Veronese, Ep. 803 (II, 478), 82.

21. Veronese, Ep. 259 (I, 404), 26; Ep. 676 (II, 261), 44.

22. Veronese, Ep. 668 (II, 217), 15.

23. Veronese, Ep. 823 (II, 522), 87.

24. Veronese, Ep. 668 (II, 217), 17.

25. Veronese, Ep. 777 (II, 420), 213.

26. Cf. Augusto Campana, "Una Lettera Inedita di Guarino Veronese e il Plutarco Mediceo della Bottega di Vespasiano," *Italia medioevale e umanistica* V (1962) p. 177.

27. Veronese, Ep. 796 (II, 460), 73.

28. Veronese, Ep. 706 (II, 310), 52.

29. Veronese, Ep. 223 (I, 356), 15, 57.

30. Veronese, Ep. 796 (II, 462), 142.

31. Veronese, Ep. 66 (I, 137), 60.

32. Veronese, Ep. 90 (I, 167), 28.

33. Veronese, Ep. 803 (II, 478), 81.

34. Veronese, Ep. 580 (II, 98), 12.

35. Veronese, Ep. 670 (II, 234), 459.

36. Veronese, Ep. 257 (I, 402), 6.

37. Veronese, Ep. 50 (I, 108), 18.

38. Veronese, Ep. 785 (II, 438), 45.

39. Veronese, Ep. 805 (II, 488), 44.

40. Veronese, Ep. 80 (I, 155), 17; Cicero, *De off.* I, 110.

41. Veronese, Ep. 90 (I, 167), 25.

42. Veronese, Ep. 777 (II, 415), 39.

43. Veronese, Ep. 684 (II, 278), 30.

44. Veronese, Ep. 229 (I, 364), 35.

45. Veronese, Ep. 580 (II, 105), 248.

46. Veronese, Ep. 50 (I, 108), 22.

47. Cristoforo Landino, *Disputationes Camaldulenses*, ed. Peter Lohe (Firenze: Sansoni Editore, 1980).

48. Landino, I, p. 25.

49. Landino, I, p. 26f.

50. Landino, I, p. 29.

51. Landino, III, p. 118.

52. Landino, III, p. 121. ("deduxit trepidas ramosa in compita mentes")

53. Landino, III, p. 124f.

54. Landino, III, p. 120–127.

55. Landino, III, p. 127–130.

56. Landino, III, p. 130– 138.

57. Landino, III, p. 147 f.

58. Landino, III, p. 156 f.

59. Landino, III, p. 157 ff.

60. Landino, III, p. 159 ff.

61. Landino, III, p. 166 ff.

62. Colluccio Salutati, *De nobilitate legum et medicinae*, IV, 26, ed. Eugenio Garin (Firenze: Vallecchi Editore, 1947).

63. Salutati, 4, 27.

64. Salutati, 6, 1.

65. Salutati, 6, 11.

66. Salutati, 6, 8.

67. Salutati, 6, 18.
68. Salutati, 160, 15.
69. Salutati, 162, 25.
70. Salutati, 12, 29.
71. Salutati, 90, 14.
72. Salutati, 90, 20.
73. Salutati, 14, 11.
74. Salutati, 14, 26; 16, 11.
75. Salutati, 16, 11.

Notes to Chapter 4

1. Immanuel Kant, *Reflexionen zur Anthropologie, Akademie Ausgabe*, vol. XV/I, § 991.

2. Hegel, *Grundlinien der Philosophie des Rechts* (Berlin, 1821: Hamburg, 1967), p. 14.

3. J. L. Vives, *De disciplinis*, Liber IV, Caput IV, *Opera omnia* T. VI, (Valentiae, 1785), p. 171. (rpt. 1964: London, Gregg Press Ltd.), p. 171, emphasis mine.

4. Vives, "Praefatio," T. VI, p. 5.

5. Vives, *De tradendis*, I, 1, T. VI, p. 243.

6. Vives, *De causis*, T. VI, p. 8.

7. *De causis*, V, 1, T. VI, p. 181.

8. ". . . quidquid nunc est in artibus, in natura prius fuit, non aliter quam uniones in conchae aut gemmae in arena." Vives, *De tradendis*, I, 2, T. VI, p. 250.

9. "Prima rerum inventio necessitati succurrit; haec enim ingenia mirifice exacuit ad ea excudenda, quibus obsessor adeo gravis arceatur." *De causis*, I, 1, T. VI, p. 8.

10. *De causis*, I, 2, T. VI, p. 13.

11. *De causis*, I, 2, T. VI, p. 14.

12. *De causis*, V, 1, T. VI, p. 181.

13. *De causis*, I, 2, T. VI, p. 15.

14. Praef., T. VI, p. 5.

15. Virgil, *Georgics* II, 177. *The Works of Vergil* (Hildesheim: Georg Olms, 1963), V. 1, "Eclogues and Georgics," ed. F. Haverfield, p. 242.

16. Ovid, *Metamorphoses* III, 159.

17. Statius, *Silvae* I, 3, 15 ff. p. 37; II, 3, 58 p. 110. Tr. J. Mozley (Cambridge, MA: Loeb, 1961).

18. *Georgics* I, 415, p. 214.

19. *Georgics* II, 382, p. 265.

20. Ovid, *Tristia* V, 10, 18. Tr. Arthur Wheeler (Cambridge: Loeb, 1939), p. 246; *Epistulae ex Ponto* II, 1, 52 p. 246; IV, 7, 22.

21. "... quaeque diu latuere." *Metamorphoses* XV, 147.

22. *Epistulae ex Ponto* II, 5, 21 p. 342; *Tristia* IV, 4, 17, p. 178.

23. "Oracula mentis." *Metamorphoses* XV, 145.

24. Cicero, *Tusculanae disput.* I, 16, *Opera* IV, 219–220.

25. *Tusc. Disp.* I, 25, 63, *Opera,* IV, p. 220.

26. "... *vis intuendi* ... seu *acumen.*" Vives, *De tradendis,* I, 5, T. VI, p. 262.

27. "... *vis* quaedam *judicandi,* ac *statuendi.*" *De tradendis,* I, 5., T. VI, p. 262.

28. "... dedit natura homini sensus in corpore; in animo vero acumen, quo cernat, speculetur, intelligat, apprehendat; tum judicium, quo sparsa et dissipata velut indagine quadam colligat." *De causis,* V. 2, T. VI, p. 185.

29. *De causis,* I, 2, T. VI, p. 250.

30. *De causis,* II, 6. T. VI, p. 250.

31. "Acre ingenium, et usui aptum, naturae sunt munera." *De causis,* I, 2, T. VI, p. 15.

32. *De causis,* I, 2, T. VI, p. 15.

33. "... diligentia, vel necessitate urgetur, vel delectatione allicitur, vel admiratione magnitudinis et pulchritudinis rei capitur." *De causis,* I, 2, T. VI, p. 15.

34. "... homines perfuncti domesticis, et necessariis negotiis, applicent animum ad aliquid altius ac liberalius cognoscendum, ita artibus, quae praesenti atque urgenti necessitati opem ferrent, rite inventis ac constitutis, visum est humano ingenio sensim ad pulchriora sese attollere." *De causis,* I, 1, T. VI, p. 9.

35. *De causis,* I, 2, T. VI, p. 14.

36. "His partis, riteque constitutis, transiit humana mens a necessitatibus ad commoditates, ut, inventis illis, haberet non solum quo se a tanta et tam continua violentia tueretur, sed jucundum quiddam, quo etiam post depulsam necessitatem juvaretur." *De tradendis,* I, 1, T. VI, p. 246.

37. *De tradendis,* I, 1, T. VI, p. 8.

38. "Deus tamen instrumentum ei reliquit ad eas quoque modo propulsandas *Ingenii acumen vivax, et sua sponte actuosum:* hic sunt nata inventa hominum." *De tradendis,* I, 1, T. VI, p. 8.

39. *De anima et vita,* II, 7, T. III, p. 372.

40. *De censura,* T. III, p. 143.

41. *De tradendis,* I, I, T. VI, p. 245.

42. "De censura veri," T. III, p. 142.

43. "Epistola Nuncupatoria," T. II, p. 89.

44. *De causis,* IV, I, T. VI, p. 152.

45. *De disciplinis,* II, 10, T. VI, p. 153.

46. "Ego vero aio atque affirmo, et ita affirmo ut nihil aliud preter hanc bonum esse contendam." L. Valla, *De vero falsoque bono,* ed. Maristella Lorch (New York, 1977), p. 34.

47. Valla I, 15, 1. See: Cicero, *De finibus* II, 1, 3. vol. IV, p. 106.

48. ". . . quid magis vitam conservat quam voluptas?" Ibid., I, 35, 1.
49. Valla, I, 5, 8.
50. Valla, I, 5, 2.
51. Valla, I, 33, 1.
52. Valla, III, 4, 2.
53. Valla, I, 5, 2.
54. Cicero, *De finibus* II, 14, 45. vol IV, p. 109.
55. Valla, I, 1, 9.
56. Valla, II, 1–2.
57. Valla, II, 19, 61.
58. Valla, I, 33, 2.
59. Valla, I, 35, 1.
60. Valla, I, 35, 1.
61. ". . . nec modo non novit quid superiores fecerint sed ne curat quidem nosse, aut, si novit, vel male judicat vel non multum miratur." Valla, II, 9, 10.
62. Valla, II, 9, 11.
63. Valla, II, 1, 4.
64. "Ego isto consilio nullum unquam audivi absurdius. Quid hoc sibi vult se sibi premium esse? Fortiter faciam. Cur? Propter honestatem. Quid est honestas? Fortiter facere. Ludus videtur hic esse non preceptum, iocus non admonitio. Fortiter faciam ut fortiter faciam, ad mortem ibo ut moriar. Hoccine est premium, heccine remuneratio? Nonne liquido fateris honestatem imaginariam rem esse que nullum exitum potest invenire?" Valla, II, 1, 9.
65. Aristotle, *Nicomachean Ethics* II, 6–8, 1107a.
66. Valla, III, 4, 7.
67. "Quid duas res unam facis?" Valla, III, 4, 7.
68. "Quid unum verbum in duas significationes ultra quam ferat eius natura diducis? Quid aliis vocabulis suam potestatem adimis, aliis donas non suam?" Valla, III, 4, 7.
69. Valla, III, 4, 8.
70. Valla, III, 4, 8.
71. Valla, II, 15, 6.
72. "Melius itaque singulos actus ac singulas res iudicamus. Eadem hora ero subinde temperatus et intemperatus, prope dixerim milies et milies eadem hora recte aut secus facere possum; adeo unicum verbum laudari vel vituperari solet." Valla, III, 4, 9.
73. Valla, III, 4, 15.
74. "Siquidem philosophia velut miles est aut tribunus sub imperatrice oratione et ut magnus quidam tragicus appellat regina." Valla, I. 10, 3.
75. Valla, I, 10, 2.
76. ". . . et si qui repugnassent, gladium illum quem a regina rerum eloquen-

tia acceperat in latrunculos philosophos strinxisset et male meritos male mulctasset." Valla, I, 10, 3.

77. Cf. Cicero, *De oratore*, 3, 31, 125: "Rerum . . . copia verborum copiam gignit." *Opera*, vol I. p. 316. Quintilian, VIII.

78. "Precipue rem perspicuam facit et ponit ante oculos." Ibid., II, Proem. I.

79. Valla, III, Proem. 1.

80. Valla, III, Proem. 1.

81. Valla, III, Proem. 3.

82. Valla, III, Proem. 1.

83. Valla, I, 13, 5.

84. Paul, Rom. 14, 23.

85. Paul, Rom. 1, 17.

86. Valla, III, 8, 1. Paul, Heb, 11, 6.

87. Valla, III, 8, 2.

88. Valla, III, 13, 2.

89. Valla, III, 9, 3.

90. Valla, III, 10, 1.

91. Luke 18, 30; Matthew 19, 29. Ibid., III, 10, 2.

92. Valla, I, 2, 3.

93. Valla, II, 28, 1.

94. Aristotle, *Nicomachean Ethics* X, 7, 1177a, and X, 8, 1178a.

95. Plato, *Philebus*, 36c–38; *Republic* IX, 580 d; Aristotle, *Nicomachean Ethics* I, 1095, b 15.

96. Valla, II, 28, 5.

97. Valla, II, 28, 9.

98. Valla, II, 28, 11.

99. "Et nihilominus stolidissimum est, cum deorum formam habitumque atque adeo substantiam ingenio consequi nequeamus, audere de ipsorum vite administratione pronuntiare, veluti si quis non ignarus elephantum et formicam esse animalia, nescius cuiusmodi et qualia animalia sint, velit tamen que sit illorum vite actio divinare." Valla, II 28, 13.

100. Cicero, *De officiis* III, IX, 39. *Opera*, IV, p. 718.

101. Plato, *Republic* II, 359–360. Ed. James Adam (Cambridge: At the University Press, 1969), p. 69.

102. ". . . cum nullum ex historiis possitis recitare exemplum, *ad fabulas* confugitis." Valla, II, 26, 1.

Notes to Chapter 5

1. Aristotle, *De anima*, 431, b 2.

2. *De Anima*, 431 a 16.

3. Erasmus, *Moriae Encomium, Opera omnia* (Amsterdam: North Holland Publishing Company, 1974), vol. IV, p. 68.

4. Sophocles, *Ajax*, v. 594.

5. Euripides, *Hippolytus*, v. 966.

6. Jeremiah 5, 21.

7. I. Cor. 1, 25.

8. M. Luther, *Die ganze Heilige Schrift*, Deutsch (Wittenberg, 1545), ed. H. Volz (München, 1972), p. 8.

9. Erasmus, p. 74.

10. Erasmus, p. 112.

11. Erasmus, p. 78. Cf. also Homer, *Odyssey* IX, 109.

12. Erasmus, p. 134.

13. Erasmus, p. 134.

14. Erasmus, p. 82.

15. Erasmus, p. 84.

16. Erasmus, 14, 29.

17. Erasmus, p. 84.

18. Ovid, *Metamorphoses* I, 452; XI, 410; IV, 571.

19. Erasmus, p. 106.

20. Erasmus, p. 90.

21. Erasmus, p. 106 ("marmoreum hominis simulacrum").

22. Erasmus, p. 80.

23. Erasmus, p. 80.

24. Erasmus, p. 80.

25. Erasmus, p. 80.

26. Erasmus, p. 74.

27. Erasmus, p. 23, 27, 42, 43.

28. Erasmus, p. 118.

29. Erasmus, p. 104.

30. Erasmus, p. 130.

31. Erasmus, p. 116.

32. Erasmus, p. 118.

33. Erasmus, p. 132.

34. Erasmus, p. 118.

35. Allen, P. S. ed. *Opus epistolarum Desiderii Erasmi* (Oxford: Clarendon Press, 1910), T. II, p. 12, Ep. 304.

36. Erasmus, *Opera omnia*, Leyden 1703–1706, IX, 1094–1196.

37. *Opera*, 36, 84.

38. Alberti, *Momus*, ed. G. Martini (Bologna, 1942), p. 5.

39. Alberti.

40. Alberti, p. 16.

41. Alberti, p. 16.

42. Alberti, p. 16.

43. Alberti, p. 17.

44. Alberti, p. 18.

45. Alberti, p. 20.

46. Alberti, p. 40.

47. Alberti, p. 25.

48. Alberti. p. 25.

49. Alberti, p. 41.

50. Alberti, p. 40.

51. Alberti, p. 43.

52. Alberti, p. 43.

53. Alberti, p. 44.

54. Leonardo, C. A. 119 v. a. The following references are contained in *The Literary Works of Leonardo Da Vinci*, ed. Jean Paul Richter (New York: Phaidon, 1970), 2 vols.; abbreviations are keyed to MSS. numbers.

55. Leonardo, C. A. 119, v. a., vol. I, p. 116.

56. Leonardo, C. A. 119, v. a., vol. I, p. 116.

57. Leonardo, C. A. 119, v. a., vol. I, p. 116.

58. Leonardo, C. A. 191, r. a.

59. Leonardo, C. A. 117 r. b.

60. Leonardo, C. A. 86 r. a. p. 240.

61. Leonardo, For. III, 43 v.

62. Leonardo, Triv. 33 v.

63. Leonardo, An. 1, 13. v.

64. Leonardo, Lu. 1.

65. Leonardo, M. 58 v.

66. Leonardo, J. 18 r. a.

67. Leonardo, Lu. 1.

68. Leonardo, An. II, 14 r (W 19084).

69. Alberti, p. 131.

70. Alberti, p. 113.

71. Alberti, p. 114.

72. Alberti, p. 120.

73. Alberti, p. 133.

74. Alberti, p. 135.

75. Alberti, p. 135.

76. Alberti, p. 135.

77. Alberti, p. 57.

78. Alberti, p. 83.

79. Alberti, p. 85–86.

80. Alberti, p. 57–58.
81. Alberti, p. 69.
82. Alberti, p. 70.
83. Alberti, p. 75.
84. Alberti, p. 71.
85. Cf. Episode of Enopus, p. 151.
86. Alberti, p. 176.
87. Alberti, p. 186.
88. Alberti, p. 187.

Notes to Chapter 6

1. Cf. O. Pöggeler, "Hegel, der Verfasser des ältesten Systemprogramms des deutschen Idealismus," in *Hegel-Studien*, Beiheft 4, 1969, p. 17.
2. Hölderlin, *Sämtliche Werke*, ed. F. Beissner, Frankfurt a. M. 1961, p. 1014–1016. *Mythologie der Vernunft. Hegels "ältestes Systemprogramm" des deutschen Idealismus*, ed. Chr. Jamme und H. Schneider (Frankfurt: Suhrkamp, 1984), pp. 11–14.
3. *Systemprogramm*, p. 13.
4. *Systemprogramm*, p. 13.
5. Aristotle, *Met.* IV, 3, 1005 b 5.
6. Dante, *De vulgari eloquentia* I, IV, p. 48.
7. L. Bruni, *Rerum suo tempore gestarum commentarius, Rerum italicarum Scriptores*, Tom. XIX, 3, 432.
8. Cristoforo Landino, *Disputationes Camaldulenses*, Bk. 4.
9. *Reden des Cristoforo Landino*, ed. M. Lentzen (München, 1974), p. 25, 110.
10. *Reden*, p. 25, 100.
11. *Reden*, p. 24, 77.
12. *Reden*, p. 24, 79.
13. Marsilio Ficino, *Theologia Platonica*, I, 1 (Torino: Bottega d'Erasmo, 1962), facs. rpt of Basil 1576 ed., p. 107.
14. Ficino, I, 2, 108.
15. Ficino, p. 108.
16. Ficino, X, 3, p. 256.
17. Ficino, I, 2, p. 109.
18. Ficino, I, 3, p. 109.
19. Ficino, p. 109.
20. Ficino, p. 109.
21. Ficino, I, 3, p. 111.
22. Ficino, I, 3, p. 114.
23. Ficino, I, 1, p. 107.

24. Ficino, p. 107.

25. Pico della Mirandola, *Heptaplus*, in *De hominis dignitate, Heptaplus*, ed. E. Garin (Firenze, Vallechi, 1942), p. 204.

26. *Heptaplus*, p. 270.

27. Aristotle, *Met.* XII, 2, 1069; *Physics* I, 6, 189a.

28. Pico, *Heptaplus*, p. 206 (sed instrumenta potius divinae artis).

29. *Heptaplus*, p. 184.

30. *Heptaplus*, p. 186.

31. *Heptaplus*, p. 184.

32. *Heptaplus*, p. 190.

33. *Heptaplus*, p. 172.

34. *Heptaplus*, p. 172.

35. *Heptaplus*, p. 220–222.

36. *Heptaplus*, p. 302.

37. *Heptaplus*, p. 192.

38. *De hominis Dignitate*, p. 104.

39. *De hominis Dignitate*, p. 106.

40. *De hominis Dignitate*, p. 106.

41. *Heptaplus*, p. 304.

42. *De hominis dignitate*, p. 122.

43. M. F. Cattani da Diacceto, *Opere* (Venezia, 1561), p. 869.

44. Diacceto, *Opera omnia* (Basileae, 1563).

45. Diacceto, *De pulcro* III, 111, p. 77.

46. *De pulcro*, III, 111, p. 75.

47. *De pulcro*, III, 111, p. 77.

48. Diacceto, *Opere*, p. 17.

49. *Opere*, p. 17– 18.

50. Cf. also E. Grassi, *Rhetoric as Philosophy* (University Park: Pennsylvania University Press, 1980); *Heidegger and the Question of Renaissance Humanism* (Binghamton, N.Y.: MRTS, 1983); and E. Grassi and M. Lorch, *Folly and Insanity in Renaissance Literature* (Binghamton, N.Y.: MRTS, 1986).

51. Cf. Emilio Hidalgo, *Das ingeniöse Denken bei Gracian* (München: Humanistische Bibliothek, 1985).

52. *Systemprogramm*, pp. 12–14.

53. Novalis, *Schriften* (Stuttgart, 1983), vol. III, p. 410.

54. Friedrich Schlegel, *Kritische Ausgabe* (München, 1958), XVIII, p. 124.

55. Schlegel, XI, p. 92.

56. Schlegel, XII, p. 393.

57. Schlegel, XVIII, p. 252.

58. Schlegel, XII, p. 403.

59. A. W. Schlegel, *Werke* (1963), p. 82.

60. Jean Paul, *Werke*, ed. Norbert Miller (München, 1975), vol. IX, p. 171 f. Cf. "Über den Witz," IX, p. 169–207. Cf. E. Grassi, *Macht der Phantasie* (1979) pp. 177–184.

61. F. W. J. Schelling, *Werke*, 1856, Abt. I, III, p. 626, 627.

62. John Neubauer, *Symbolismus und Symbolische Logik* (München: Wilhelm Fink Verlag, 1978), p. 215.

mRts

meðieual & Renaissance texts & stuðies
is the publishing program of the
Center for Medieval and Early Renaissance Studies
State University of New York at Binghamton.

mRts emphasizes books that are needed —
texts, translations, and major research tools.

mRts aims to publish the highest quality scholarship
in attractive and durable format at modest cost.